Ethics for the Property-Casualty Insurance Professional

**Dearborn
R&R Newkirk**
a division of Dearborn Financial Publishing, Inc.

While a great deal of care has been taken to provide accurate and current information, the ideas, suggestions, general principles and conclusions presented in this text are subject to local, state and federal laws and regulations, court cases and any revisions of same. The reader thus is urged to consult legal counsel regarding any points of law?this publication should not be used as a substitute for competent legal advice.

This text is updated periodically to reflect changes in laws and regulations. To verify that you have the most recent update, you may call Dearborn • R&R Newkirk at 1-800-432-4723.

Project Editor: Sheryl A. Lilke
Interior Design: Lucy Jenkins
Cover Design: DePinto Studios

© 1994 by Dearborn Financial Publishing, Inc.

Published by Dearborn • R&R Newkirk,
a division of Dearborn Financial Publishing, Inc.

All rights reserved. The text of this publication, or any part thereof, may not be reproduced in any manner whatsoever without written permission from the publisher.

Printed in the United States of America.

First Printing, October 1994

Ethics for the property / casualty professional.
    p. cm.
  ISBN 0-7931-1196-X
    1. Insurance agents—Professional ethics—United States.
  2. Property insurance agents—United States. 3. Casualty insurance agents—United States. I. Dearborn•R&R Newkirk.
HG8091.E86 1994   94-31602
  174' .9368—dc20   CIP

Table of Contents

ACKNOWLEDGMENTS	v
INTRODUCTION	vii

CHAPTER 1
ETHICS: PRINCIPALS AND PRACTICES — 1

Understanding Ethics	1
Ethics for Insurance Agents	8
Ethics for Insurance Brokers	10
Primary Characteristics of a Profession	11
Ethical Issue Number One: "Unauthorized Knowledge"	15

CHAPTER 2
RESPONSIBILITIES TO THE INSURER — 17

The Concept of Agency	17
Authority of an Agent	19
The Agent as a Fiduciary	21
Duties of the Principal to the Agent	25
Who Is an Agent of the Insurer?	26
Serving the Insurer Serves the Consumer	27
Ethical Issue Number Two: "I'll Gladly Pay You Tuesday . . ."	28

CHAPTER 3
RESPONSIBILITIES TO THE CONSUMER — 31

Property-Casualty Insurance Coverage	31
Property-Casualty Insurance Marketing Systems	32
An Agent's Duties and Responsibilities	33
Selling to Needs	35
Providing Service to Clients	39
Risk Management	41
Building a Tradition	45
Ethical Issue Number Three: "Mis-App"	46

CHAPTER 4
RESPONSIBILITIES TO THE GENERAL PUBLIC — 49

The Need for Insurance	49
Issues Facing Insurers	53
Issues Facing Insurance Producers	56
Public Perceptions of the Insurance Industry	58
Ethical Issue Number Four: "Elementary, My Dear Watson…"	61

CHAPTER 5
ETHICS AND THE LAW — 63

How the Insurance Industry Is Regulated	63
Consumer Protection	65
License Suspension/Termination	70
Personal Values and Ethics	70
Corporate Ethics	72
Ethical Issue Number Five: "Package 1 or Package 2"	76

CHAPTER 6
PRACTICAL ANSWERS TO ETHICAL QUESTIONS — 79

Ethical Decision Making	79
Practical Ways to Avoid Trouble	84
Guidelines for Ethical Decision Making	88
Ethical Issue Number Six: "Housewarming"	90

GUIDELINES TO ETHICAL ISSUES — 93

Ethical Issue Number One	94
Ethical Issue Number Two	95
Ethical Issue Number Three	97
Ethical Issue Number Four	99
Ethical Issue Number Five	101
Ethical Issue Number Six	102

Codes of Ethics — 103

Independent Insurance Agents of America	104
Code of Ethics: American Institute for Chartered Property Casualty Underwriters	105

Acknowledgments

Our sincere thanks to the following individuals who helped develop this text through their thoughtful reviews, comments and suggestions.

Jeff Galper, Branch Manager
Dearborn Financial Institute, Southfield, Michigan

Elizabeth C. Goldin
FLMI, Adjunct Professor of Risk Management and Insurance
Moorehouse College, Atlanta, Georgia

David Roseman, Adjunct Professor and Instructor
Academic and Corporate Management Training, Denver, Colorado

Phillip B. Rosen, CIC, Vice President
Insurance Service Center, Skokie, Illinois

Introduction

Welcome to *Ethics for the Property-Casualty Professional!* As you open the cover, you probably have some important questions about this course, such as: *"What's the basic purpose of this course?" "What will it do for me?" "If I already feel that I'm an ethical person, why should I take this course?"* Before you go any further—before any of those questions can impede your concentrating on the subject matter that follows—let's answer them.

■ ■ ■ ■ ■

First, *what is the basic purpose of this course?* The purpose of this course is twofold. First, under the law of torts, professionals have long been held to higher standards of care than nonprofessionals. Therefore, every insurance producer faces growing proof for continuing competence after obtaining his or her various insurance licenses. Many states now require (or are considering) mandatory continuing education and training in ethics—a requirement that this course addresses. Second, this text addresses the complexities of ethical decision making in today's insurance environment. It suggests ways for property-casualty producers to establish ethics in the workplace and thereby take a step toward reducing the possibility of questionable practices and wrongdoing.

Second, *what will this course do for you?* This course will not provide answers for every moral dilemma that property-casualty producers face. There simply are no clear-cut definitive answers to every predicament producers encounter. What this text *does* provide is a set of theoretical tools that will assist producers to sensitively and intelligently face (or possibly prevent) ethical dilemmas by identifying the variables that make up the problem, deciding on an acceptable solution and then acting so that solution is achieved quickly and efficiently.

Third, *if you're already an ethical person, why should you take this course?* This course is a balanced presentation of a property-casualty producer's agency relationships and relationships with policyowners, the public, the state and the insurance industry. Perhaps the best reason for taking this course is to reinforce your professional competence by examining and responding to a variety of ethical issues relating to those relationships. We end each chapter with an ethical issue. Study the situation carefully and develop your own answer about how you would deal with the issue. Once you have developed your answer, you may then wish to refer to the back of the book where we have included our own ethical answer.

It is our sincere hope that you will enjoy your study of *Ethics for the Property-Casualty Professional* and that, because of it, you will grow personally and professionally.

Diane M. Lamyotte, CPCU, AU
Editor

1

Ethics: Principles and Practices

The purpose of this course is to provide the foundation of knowledge and understanding an individual needs to function ethically in his or her role as a property-casualty insurance professional. Our concentration will be on the social, professional and legal aspects of ethics. Also discussed is how each of these broad areas of ethical responsibility influences the insurance agent's activities. We'll begin by discussing the concept of ethics in general.

UNDERSTANDING ETHICS

Human beings, like all other animals, are born with primary survival instincts. These instincts—the desire to obtain food, shelter and safety—develop long before our questions about what constitutes ethical behavior. As with all philosophical studies, the difficulty in understanding ethics is due to one very simple cause: we attempt to find answers without first discovering precisely what questions we want to ask.

Most of us are told from early childhood that we should not cheat, steal, bribe or accept bribes. This is simple everyday honesty. However, it seems that almost every day we hear about insider trading, judicial bribery, contractor payoffs or tax cheating. And, although many insurance agents would like to believe differently, the insurance industry is not immune to dishonesty. Almost every day some insurance company or insurance agent receives negative publicity as a result of bad judgment or poor ethical conduct. Because bad news usually attracts far more attention than good news, this is not surprising. What is significant is the lack of attention paid to the legions of property-casualty insurance professionals who perform their daily sales and service tasks in a thoughtful and ethical manner. Their accomplishments have provided the inspiration for this chapter and those that follow.

Ethics Defined

Ethics is a derivative of the Greek words *ethikos*, meaning "moral" and *ethos*, meaning "character." By textbook definition, ethics is "a branch of philosophy that deals with the values of human life in a coherent, systematic and scientific manner." *The Oxford English Dictionary* defines ethics as "the department of study concerned with the principles of human duty" and the "rules of conduct recognized in certain associations or departments of human life." *Webster's Third International Dictionary* defines ethics as "the discipline dealing with what is good and bad or right and wrong or with moral duty and obligation."

As you will discover throughout this text, the subject of ethics can be studied on two levels:

1. *on the philosophical level*—where careful reflection enables you to meet trouble calmly and rationally while increasing your personal efficiency as an insurance professional; and

2. *on the practical level*—where a code of ethics helps you gain personal and professional satisfaction and also helps you avoid controversy and misunderstandings with your insurers and clients.

Ethics and Philosophy

You will not find universal agreement among philosophers as to what in all cases is ethically correct. For example, early Greek philosophers saw man as a tragic hero, expressing the best that man could be. Their philosophy was somewhere between the depressing hopelessness of earlier Eastern societies and the later hope-filled promises of the higher religions. There was not, as in Judaism, the promise of the Covenant; nor, as in Christianity, the assurance of the Resurrection; nor, as in Islam, the rewards for those who obey the Koran. Essentially, many of the early Greek philosophers saw the fulfillment of human life *simply in the living of life*. For example, Aeschylus (525–456 B.C.), the leading writer and poet of his generation, placed an emphasis on courage and idealism. He offered man the nobility, often magnificent, of a lost cause.

Socrates believed that there is never a good reason or excuse for doing wrong. To the usual questions of "What will other people think?" or "What would other people do?" Socrates replied that he made up his own mind and lived by his own dictates. Moreover, because he had a fairly low opinion of people, Socrates considered his moral decisions superior to those of other people. He chose to do what was right not to win him friends or to help him succeed. He did right for its own sake—an old idea that has been restated in countless ways: Virtue is its own reward.

Many religious philosophers have argued that ethics cannot exist without religion. They say *right* is determined by the will of God, and *wrong* is anything contrary to God's will. Traditionally the link between religion and ethics provides a reason for doing what is right: Those who are moral in this life will be rewarded with eternal happiness; those who are immoral will be condemned to eternal damnation. This reasoning also assumes that religion contributes to social order: People will be "good" to avoid punishment or to win social approval; if they are "bad," they will be punished in this life, in the afterlife, or perhaps in both.

However, not all religious thinkers have accepted this premise. Immanuel Kant, a German philosopher, rejected the Christian belief of rewards and punishments. He believed that moral law should be obeyed for its own sake, not because one will be rewarded for obeying or punished for disregarding it. Kant argued that rational human beings have *autonomy,* or the ability to choose, make and act on their own decisions. Kant stated that because people are rational and can choose among alternatives, they are likely to make the proper moral choices and to act ethically. The most obvious reason for avoiding unethical behavior is *not* fear of punishment; it is that our personal and professional success are determined in large part by who we are—by our beliefs, values, character and ethics. Being ethical isn't a question of just *knowing* what's right or wrong; it's a matter of *doing* what's right.

Ethics and Practicality

Are there any practical reasons for a person to choose to be moral and ethical? Some people would argue that today's fast-paced, competitive society prevents people from telling the truth all the time. Some people feel that special rules apply to business and that personal ethics must be set aside when business is involved. For example, every property-casualty insurance agent faces vigorous competition from other agents when soliciting, servicing and renewing accounts. From time to time most agents feel compelled, in the interest of their insurers or themselves, to practice some form of deception when negotiating with clients, government units or their own insurance companies. They may feel pressured to make conscious misstatements, conceal pertinent facts or exaggerate a situation to persuade others to purchase insurance coverage. It simply isn't *practical*, they say, to allow someone else to make the sale, even if they have to overstate the difference between the two products. How do insurance agents reconcile the need to make a sale to earn their income with their own personal sense of ethics?

Ethics does not have to be incompatible with business success; after all, most businesses are formed as profit-seeking organizations and "profit" is not a dirty word. In fact, in the long run, good ethics is good business. Most clients prefer to work with an ethical insurance agent, someone they can trust.

Acting ethically does not mean you should step aside and allow a usually less successful agent make the sale. What it does require is an understanding of what is important to you as an insurance professional. You may think that it is appropriate to disregard your sense of personal ethics when you are conducting business. You may feel you are moral in your personal dealings, but that "everyone cheats and lies to get ahead in business," so you should, too. If you believe that your only goal is to sell insurance, regardless of what you have to say or do to accomplish your goal, you clearly are able to set your personal ethics aside when business is involved.

However, if you have high standards of honesty and personal integrity, you may be unable to compromise them, even if your agency or client asks you to do so. Assume you have the opportunity to provide an insurance quotation for Bob's Salvage, a large commercial account. After you provide Bob with a competitive quote, he tells you that his current agent gives him a "finder's fee" of 10 percent of the annual premium. If you want the account, you'll have to do the same. Regardless of what Bob or his agent call it, "finder's fees" are rebates and are illegal in your state. You have no control over the conduct of others, only over your own. As an ethical agent, you decline to write the account. The reason for your choice can be summarized by Mark Twain's famous quote: "Always do right. This will gratify some people, and astonish the rest."

Beliefs and Values

Faced with a choice between doing what they think is right and what they think is wrong, of course, people *should* do what they think is moral or ethical. But how do they learn to choose what is right? Moral behavior as well as moral judgment are dependent on the formation of a strong moral *conscience* that is often originally developed by parental surveillance and threats of punishment. As people get older, they develop their own powerful belief systems and values that may or may not reflect their parents' beliefs and values.

Beliefs are those convictions or sentiments that we assume to be true. A belief system is formed by a person's interpretation of and response to various life experiences. People's beliefs influence their choices, their decisions and their life directions. People sometimes act on beliefs without testing their validity, because beliefs can become synonymous with facts in their minds. For example, if you believe that people are generally honest, you are likely to believe a coworker's excuse for a late report. However, if you believe that people are generally lazy, you will interpret a late report as proof of your beliefs, regardless of the excuse you hear.

In addition to beliefs, human beings have values that influence who they are, what they stand for and by what guidelines they live. *Values* are ideals that affect a person's decisions about which principles or qualities are most worthwhile. For example, assume that Cathy, a member of a college admissions staff, believes in the equality of all human beings. She rejects all forms of racial, sexual or ethnic discrimination. The college wants to increase the number of minority students in its medical program and considers reserving 20 out of every 100 places for students belonging to a minority group. When asked to vote on the proposed admissions procedure, Cathy must determine whether this policy of reverse discrimination, which can actually help minority groups, is justified. Her response to the situation answers a basic question, "What do I stand for?" Or to quote Anton Chekhov, "Man is what he believes."

A person chooses his or her beliefs and values in a number of ways. When people are very young, they tend to take the word of someone in *authority* (a parent, a teacher, a friend) that something is "good," "bad," "right," "wrong," etc. As people grow older, they also rely on *logic* ("Since A is true, B must be true, because B follows A"), their own *senses* ("I saw Mary kicking her dog so she must be a bad person"), *emotions* ("All foreigners should be expelled from America") and *intuition* ("I wasn't sure what to do so I slept on it and in the morning I knew exactly what to do"). By choosing to rely on authority, personal observation and so forth, people create their own value systems or personal codes of ethics that guide their actions and determine what kind of people they are or can become.

Honesty and Ethics

Human beings have the extraordinary power of choice—to choose to be good or evil, to be generous or self-centered, to be immoral or ethical. Honesty is the basis of ethics and relates to a person's integrity and truthfulness. In his *Farewell*

Address, George Washington echoed Miguel de Cervantes when he said, "I hold the maxim no less applicable to public than to private affairs, that honesty is the best policy." As most individuals know, when we are less than honest, we suffer some guilt or responsibility for the wrongdoing. Some experts argue that, apart from the wrong we are each responsible for personally, in a sense no wrong is done anywhere that we are not all responsible for collectively. With or without knowing it, through what we have done or what we have failed to do, we have all helped to create the kind of world mess that makes wrongdoing inevitable. From where does such thinking come?

Throughout history philosophers and religious leaders have expressed the need for humans to treat one another fairly and honestly. The almost universal view that human beings should go beyond their own personal interests and behave honorably toward others—the so-called *Golden Rule*—has been expressed in many ways. For example, in *The Confucian Analects* Confucius is quoted as saying: "What you do not want done to yourself, do not do to others." Aristotle echoes Confucius when he writes: "We should behave to our friends as we would wish our friends to behave to us." The Bible in Matthew 7:12 says: "Therefore all things whatsoever ye would that men should do to you, do ye even so to them for this is the law and the prophets." The existentialist Jean-Paul Sartré agrees, that in some sense, ethics and ethical conduct toward others are universal ideals.

Regardless of how it is phrased, the Golden Rule takes a common form: *"Do as you would be done by."* Whether taught by a parent, a teacher or a religious leader, the Golden Rule not only promises spiritual satisfaction and fulfillment, it serves as a practical guide to everyday life. When we discuss ethics, we are not dealing with a set of hard-and-fast scientific rules, but rather with attitudes, ideas and beliefs. *Ethics is really a set of instructions for a way of life*, a way for people to achieve inner peace and to live together with others in harmony.

You can easily determine whether a course of conduct is ethical by asking, "Would I want someone else to act in this manner toward me?" Failure to apply the Golden Rule will result in two separate standards of ethics, or a double standard. One standard is how you treat others; the second is how you expect others to treat you.

People should strive for a balanced and self-ordered life. These instructions revolve around a single theme: *human desires are neither right nor wrong in themselves.* The person who pursues only his or her desires, however, and avoids the painful responsibilities dictated by reason, cannot possibly know the virtue of a balanced life that makes room for both desire and reason. Although egocentric people are concerned with only their own self-interest, generous people choose higher principles—integrity, honor, decency and honesty.

The Individual and Society

The common definition of a *society* is a community bound together by common interests and standards. Socrates believed in the ideal of the *polis,* a Greek word which we translate as *city-state.* It was the creation of the polis, to the Greek mind, that marked the difference between the Greek and the barbarian. It was the polis that enabled them to live the full, intelligent and responsible lives that they wished to live. The Greek polis marked the transformation of disorderly people into a community of citizens and imposed a pattern of behavior for people without which they were unruly and vengeful, obeying only their own selfish inclinations.

In the United States, our predominant society is based on Puritanism, a creed that highlighted self-restraint and control over appetites and emotion. It was the expression of dedication to a higher ideal than self, of God-centered people awaiting direct confrontation with the Almighty. Puritanism meant community, a strong sense of earthly law and order, cooperation in establishing a social system, subordinating the individual will to social welfare. It contains a stern and demanding code of ethics that bent people not merely to the will of the state but to the higher ideal and just law of God. In essence, Puritanism provided a set of guidelines about how to deal daily with a group and a community.

However, Puritans also believed in another doctrine that almost seems the reverse side of the same coin. Puritanism has become identified with a particular set of attitudes toward success in a material sense (the Protestant work ethic) that stresses industry, thrift and achievement of wealth. Such an ethic, creating a vibrant modern capitalism that survives today, was the true safeguard of the whole economic and social order.

How Do We Define Success?

In the United States and many other countries, success is usually measured by wealth. Unfortunately, our society has become used to hearing about businesspeople who have earned their wealth through unethical, questionable or illegal activities. To many people, the term "business ethics" is an *oxymoron*—two juxtaposed concepts that result in self-contradiction, like "jumbo shrimp" or "civil war." Unfortunately, our society isn't always critical of wrongdoing and tends to think of business as inherently corrupt. In fact, many people feel that the only way to succeed in business is by cheating clients and competitors.

This tendency to emphasize personal financial gain is a common way many businesses—including the insurance industry—motivate their employees. Financial gain is often held out as the primary measure of success. This is not to say that pursuit of financial gain is wrong; however, consider how incentives such as "App-A-Day Clubs" or "Top Producers of the Month" rosters have the tendency to spotlight financial achievement while ignoring professionalism and public service. What about an agency atmosphere that stresses results by any means? Shouldn't those who have achieved ethical success—those who have best served the needs of their companies and the public—be honored too? An overemphasis on financial rewards can lead to looking at prospects on the basis of "What can I get from them?" as opposed to "What can I do for them?"

Self-interest and self-preservation are the driving forces within human beings. Without these instincts human behavior is often directionless, chaotic and self-destructive. Certainly, agents should expect to be adequately rewarded for success, and production figures are vital to the well-being of any agency or insurance company. However, the agent should remember that his or her own rewards must not be earned at the expense of the insurer, clients or general public. The wise agent will remember the advice of Polonius who says in *Hamlet*: "This above all: to thine own self be true,/And it must follow, as the night the day,/Thou canst not then be false to any man."

Ethics as a Legal Force

For some, there is a conflict because ethics deals with the way things *ought* to be—which is not necessarily practical in our society. These individuals are confused by the differences between *what is ethical* and *what is legal*, two completely separate concepts. Ethics is right for right's sake while the law represents a set of minimum standards that society demands for its survival.

Ethics usually precedes the law. While many ethical standards of conduct have been codified, many have not. So, something can be legal but not ethical. For example, it is legal to sell property insurance to a prospect that he or she does not need; however, it is not ethical. Ethics goes beyond the letter of the law and entails not only "must do" but also "should do."

However, it should be noted that the law does provide a very specific ethical direction for everyone, through civil and criminal statutes. Under the law, ethical conduct is generally defined as that which a reasonable person is expected to do under any circumstances. Also defined in the law is illegal and improper conduct, and the penalties for such conduct.

In spite of this merger of the legal and ethical, there is still a distinction between the two. How often have you heard people say, "Well, is what I've done *illegal*?" When told *"no,"* they assume that their actions must then be acceptable. Misleading advertising, questionable management procedures and gifts to obtain business may not always be illegal but they may be unethical. The integrity and truthfulness of a company's policies are subject to scrutiny by the general public. Public pressure may force a business to revise its practices. What this means is that what is legal today, but unethical, could become illegal tomorrow, depending upon pressure by the community to bring about reform.

However, relying on legalities alone can become the easy way out. Paying attention to "have-to" rules and regulations at the expense of "choose-to" ethical standards can keep the individual out of legal trouble, but may also result in a delusion of success. Ethics has more to do with approval from the man or woman in the mirror than it does with approval from one's employer or the insurance companies one represents.

The Ideal Path

The old question, "Would you want your decision to appear on the front page of tomorrow's edition of *The New York Times*?" still holds true. If the answer is *"no,"* then you've made some errors in judgment. In other words, the ideal path for the ethical insurance agent is to follow his or her own conscience. The ability to greet one's own face in the mirror each morning and be able to stare back at it without shame or embarrassment is priceless.

When you are about to lie for any reason, you might probe your own reasons for doing so and analyze their implications. One simple way to test yourself is to ask, "What will I tell my child or spouse or friend when he or she asks me why I did that?" If the answer presents problems for you, you may have violated your own sense of right and wrong.

In our modern society it may be difficult for many individuals to live in an absolutely ethical manner. But, although the ideal may be unachievable, you should always strive for it. Thomas Watson, chief executive officer of IBM, once said,

"If you reach for a star you will never get a star, but neither will you get a handful of mud."

The fact is that life today is infinitely more ethical in many respects than at any previous age. We have simply created more and higher ethical standards than in the past. For example, we no longer permit wealthy people to buy their way out of compulsory military service in time of war, although this was once considered perfectly ethical and proper. Indeed, there is room to believe that what seems to be a decline in ethics is actually a rise in acceptable standards.

ETHICS FOR INSURANCE AGENTS

An insurance *agent* is anyone who solicits insurance or who aids in the placing of risks, delivery of policies or collection of premiums on behalf of an insurance company. The acts of agents are binding upon the company only to the extent specified in their contracts or otherwise authorized to do so. Agents cannot delegate their rights or powers unless expressly authorized. In most states, insurance solicitors are regarded as agents of the insurance company and not of the insured. Agents act in a *fiduciary* capacity and occupy a position of special trust and confidence, as in handling or supervising the affairs or funds of another. As a test of your understanding of your role, ask yourself these questions:

Is it ethical for an insurance agent to take the names of individuals who registered for a supermarket drawing out of the barrel and use them for a prospect list?

Is it ethical for an insurance agent to call himself or herself a risk manager without the proper training, experience or qualifications?

Is it ethical for an insurance agent to pose as a hazard inspector just to get in a house to make a homeowners insurance presentation?

The answer to all of these questions is *"no."* None of these situations shows proper ethical behavior by an insurance agent. However extreme these examples might seem, they represent ethical responsibilities that an insurance agent is expected to fulfill. An agent's four primary ethical responsibilities are

1. to the agent's insurer;

2. to the agent's policyowners;

3. to the general public; and

4. to the state.

Each of these areas will be discussed in detail in the following chapters, but let's take a brief look now.

Ethical Responsibilities to the Insurer

The duties of an insurance agent to his or her insurer are established by the concept of *agency*. This concept is tangibly represented by the agency contract, which both parties agree to and sign. As representatives of insurance companies, agents may be granted wide authority: to inspect risks; to immediately bind an insurer by oral or written agreement; to issue various types of contracts; to collect premiums due, etc. Within the scope of that contract, the insurance agent owes to his or her insurer the duties of honesty, good faith and loyalty. He or she also is obligated to reveal to the insurer all material facts concerning the agency relationship.

In carrying out his or her duties, the insurance agent is the direct representative of the insurer. His or her day-to-day activities are a direct reflection on the insurer's image within the community. Consequently, the agent is obligated to do the best job possible, with sincerity, integrity and technical competency. If the agent makes promises or representations that induce the client to act on those representations, then the agent may be liable either to the client or the insurer for any damages that result. Should the agent behave unethically, everyone in that community is given reason to believe that the insurer is also unethical.

Ethical Responsibilities to Policyowners

The professional agent can meet his or her ethical responsibilities to an insured by filling needs and providing quality service. Service is a primary function of the insurance industry. The way that service is provided often determines the agent's future since clients are a good source of future sales and references.

In addition to quality service, the agent also owes the policyowner the same degree of loyalty he or she provides to the insurer. The agent is also charged with the ethical responsibilities of confidentiality, timely submission of all applications and prompt policy delivery.

Ethical Responsibilities to the General Public

The insurance agent has more control over the public's attitude toward insurance than do sales representatives for most other consumer products. This is because the insurance agent often initiates contact with a prospect, determines a prospect's need for insurance, recommends a certain product or solution, makes the sales presentation and develops a long-term relationship with after-sale service. In many cases the prospect has little or no contact with the insurance company.

Because this unique relationship involves a great deal of contact between the consumer and agent (and because the public generally understands very little about insurance), public perceptions of the insurance industry itself are based on how well—or how poorly—an agent does his or her job. Thus, the professional insurance agent has two ethical responsibilities to the public:

1. to inform the public about insurance with the highest level of professional integrity; and

2. to strive for an equally high level of professionalism in all public contacts in order to foster and maintain a strong positive image of the industry.

Ethical Responsibilities to the State

The responsibility to regulate the insurance industry is shared by the federal and state governments. However, the states carry the burden of regulating insurance affairs, including the ethical conduct of licensed insurance agents. In some states, the regulation of ethical conduct falls under the category of "marketing practices." Other states refer to it in the context of "unfair trade practices." Whatever it is called, all states have established a code of ethical standards for insurance agents by defining through laws what an agent can and cannot do. Though these laws differ from state to state, there are enough similarities to discuss them in general terms. This will be the subject of Chapter 5, in which the difference between ethics and the law will also be discussed.

■ ETHICS FOR INSURANCE BROKERS

Unlike an agent who represents an insurance company or companies, a *broker* is someone who legally represents the insured. Brokers often have specialized knowledge in many areas of insurance and act on behalf of their clients by offering them significant advice and counsel. A broker places business with more than one insurance company and has no exclusive contract requiring that all of his or her business first be offered to a single company. Although a broker does not have the authority to legally bind the insurer, he or she can solicit and accept applications and then attempt to place the coverage through an agency or with an appropriate insurer. The broker is not a party to the insurance contract as an insurer and, therefore, coverage is not effective until the insurance company receives an application and accepts the risks. (It should be noted, however, that many insurance brokers are also licensed as agents and may bind insurance coverage in their capacity as an agent.)

Agents vs. Brokers

It may be difficult for some insureds to tell the difference between an insurance agent and an insurance broker. Basically, the agent acts under specific and delegated authority from the insurer while the broker acts on behalf of the insured. Therefore, in the broker/insured relationship, the insured is considered a *principal* and the broker is considered an *agent* of the insured. Because the principal (the insured) is bound by the acts of the broker in all negotiations between the insurance company and the insured, any misrepresentation, mistake, breach of warranty or fraud committed by the broker on the insured's behalf makes the insured responsible, as if he or she had perpetrated the act.

There are many large brokerage firms, such as Alexander and Alexander, Willis Corroon and Marsh & McLennan, that play an important part in the placement of property and liability insurance. These firms often specialize in placing large, multinational corporate accounts and pride themselves on their knowledge of highly unusual insurance markets and their ability to provide risk management and loss control services.

In exchange for assisting the applicant to obtain insurance coverage, the broker (who is often an independent contractor rather than an agency or insurance company employee) receives a commission from the insurers with whom coverage is placed. To further complicate the issue, many brokers are also licensed as agents and, as such, can bind coverage, inspect risks and collect initial and renewal premiums. Because of this dual licensing, the lines between "agents" and "brokers" have blurred; many states now simply issue *insurance producer* licenses to both agents and brokers.

Excess or Surplus Lines Brokers

In insurance, an *excess lines broker* is a person licensed to place coverage not available in his or her state (or not available in a sufficient amount) through insurers not licensed to do business in the state where the broker operates. These individuals (also called *surplus lines brokers*) specialize in lines that are difficult to write, such as those that tend to have a high loss frequency (i.e., liability coverage for a public transportation system) or a severity potential (i.e., earthquake and fire following) that would strain the abilities of ordinary markets. In most cases, brokers dealing with these hard-to-place risks will seek markets such as *Lloyd's of London*, an association of individuals who have banded together to assume risks with each individual responsible only for that share of the risk he or she assumes. In other cases, coverage may be placed at higher than normal premiums with *nonadmitted insurers* that have not been licensed to do business in a particular state. Most states require excess or surplus lines carriers to be specially licensed.

The Broker's Duties

As stated, a broker's primary responsibility is to his or her client. Brokers serve their clients by finding the appropriate insurance coverages to meet the clients' needs. In addition to serving their clients, brokers are held to the same standards as agents in terms of their responsibilities to the general public. In other words, because the business of insurance requires honesty and good faith, the broker is prohibited from engaging in any marketing practice that involves unfair competition or a deceptive act. Like agents, in most states brokers are required to undertake a program of continuing eduction (CE) to remain knowledgeable and current in areas that pertain to insurance principles, coverages, laws and regulations in order to retain their license.

■ PRIMARY CHARACTERISTICS OF A PROFESSION

There has been an ongoing discussion about whether licensed insurance agents and brokers are truly *professionals* or simply individuals engaged in an *occupation*. The derivation of the word *profession* is the Latin word "professio," which means an open or public declaration. Originally the term was used only to describe those who made a public declaration of their faith by entering a religious order. Over the years the term has come to apply to a calling requiring specialized knowledge and often long academic preparation. On the other hand, the term *occupation* tends to include any work activity, especially activities that require little formal education or training, such as housekeeping, clerking or customer service.

The distinction between the terms profession and occupation escapes may people but becomes extremely important to those agents and brokers who possess more education and training, more technical knowledge and a greater commitment to the welfare of others than many so-called "professionals" in other fields. Being dismissed as merely another salesperson rather than a true professional can evoke strong emotions in some insurance circles.

Many people have tried (without much success) to clearly define the characteristics that distinguish a profession from other occupations. Many would argue that only the so-called *learned professions*—medicine, law and theology—should be regarded as true professions. However, others feel that those individuals who practice the desirable characteristics of the learned professions—such as high ethical standards, concern for the welfare of others and mandatory education and training—should also be considered professionals.

Many corporations, businesses and government units have been seeking ways to define professionalism by implementing formal *codes of conduct*, devising *mission statements* to articulate the entity's values, sponsoring training and educational programs in ethics and creating ways for employees to report illegal, unethical or questionable business practices. Despite these efforts to promote professional behavior, many experts have been unable to clearly list the characteristics that an occupation must have in order to be called a profession. For the purpose of our discussion, however, we'll look at several characteristics that are commonly considered to be the desirable traits of a profession. The following characteristics of a profession, outlined in Ronald C. Horn's text, *On Professions, Professional and Professional Ethics,* American Institute for Property and Liability Underwriters, Inc., 1978, form the basis for the CPCU code of ethics.

Commitment to High Ethical Standards

No amount of government regulation or corporate intervention can prevent some people from acting unethically or illegally. Some people clearly know the difference between right and wrong while others must be taught the difference. Those insurance professionals who have strong moral character will also have high ethical standards.

Concern for the Welfare of Others

True professionals should be more concerned with the welfare of others than with personal financial gain. Sometimes this is an easier virtue to assert than to practice because our society often defines a person's business success by the amount of money he or she earns, regardless of the means by which that wealth was accumulated. As explained earlier, many businesses—including the insurance industry—use financial rewards to motivate their employees. This does not mean that pursuit of financial gain is wrong; however, consider how incentives such as trips to exotic locales or a bonus based on written business may encourage an agent or broker to submit less-than-desirable business to an insurer in order to qualify for the incentives. Although it is possible to be a professional and provide public service while writing vast amounts of business, the producer must always be aware that he or she is serving in a fiduciary capacity. As such, special rules apply to serving the best interests of others.

The insurance business is a unique business—one that sells promises to deliver money to individuals at a future date when it will be most needed. Through the products they offer, property-casualty producers provide effective solutions to individual financial problems when a loss occurs. Although insurance professionals should be financially rewarded for their service, serving the needs of individuals and the general public is often their most meaningful reward.

Mandatory Licensing and Training

All states have laws that require insurance agents, brokers and producers to be licensed. The various state insurance departments administer these laws, with the objective of permitting only competent and honest producers to act as representatives of insurance companies. However, the standards for licensing vary widely from state to state, from simple exams to a comprehensive written examination followed by mandatory continuing education approved by the insurance department.

Many states are encouraging greater professionalism for insurance agents, brokers and producers. In recent years, numerous legislatures have passed prelicensing laws (which mandate education before insurance licensing) and continuing education laws (which mandate education after licensing and before renewal). Although the goals of the laws may be similar, implementation among the states is very dissimilar.

Prelicensing education requirements cover a full spectrum. Some states require several hours in a classroom environment, while others permit self-study courses. Mandatory continuing education requirements also vary. In some states, licensed insurance professionals may fulfill continuing education requirements for license renewal through a correspondence course or by attending an insurance seminar. Some states require detailed outlines of course content before courses are approved, while other states require affidavits certifying adherence to the law. As we will discuss in the following chapters, there is a variety of options, requirements and administrative suggestions among these alternatives.

Formal Association or Society

Many experts feel that professionals must belong to a formal association or society (either at the local or national level or both) that sets ethical standards of behavior and provides continuing education programs and publications for its members. The rationale for requiring a formal association or society is that a professional, whether a physician, attorney or an insurance producer, is part of a collective group and as such shares certain characteristics, beliefs and aspirations with other members of that group. In some sense, a formal association recognizes a sense of fellowship, which brings together individuals who share common interests, goals and educational backgrounds and who tend to speak the same technical language that is part of their chosen profession. It is this sameness that sets the group apart from all other groups and gives it a special identity.

Ability to Act with Integrity and Objectivity

Professionals should be able to act within their own personal and ethical boundaries while also acting in the best interests of their clients. This requires a great deal of sound professional skill and judgment. For example, an insurance professional should serve clients by carefully analyzing their insurance needs and selling them only the coverages that are needed. However, because an agent's income is often based entirely on commissions, he or she may be tempted to sell too much coverage or the wrong kind of coverage to clients.

In order to best serve their clients, insurance professionals must be independent from their clients. In other words, the agent must consider the needs of the client before his or her own commission or fee. In theory this is quite easy to do; however, reliance on commissions to meet one's mortgage payments and other living expenses can make overselling a tempting proposition for even the most honest agents.

Public Recognition as a Profession

Some experts contend that any occupation may be called a "profession" if the general public considers it to be one. The recognition of an occupation as a profession tends to hinge on whether it has considerable prestige, requires special skill or generates substantial income. This means that whether an individual is a medical doctor, a business executive or an NFL quarterback, that person might be considered a "professional" by the general public.

Although the general public tends to use the term "professional" loosely, most people do not consider all occupations to have the same prestige or value. For example, although there are professional sports figures who are earning millions of dollars each year, they might not be held in the same esteem as the research scientist who finds a cure for cancer. Likewise, the business executive who earned his fortune through insider trading is less likely to be considered a professional than the lawyer engaged in civil rights litigation. Therefore, the worth of a career or profession might be judged by the ethical standards to which its members are held.

If insurance agents wish to be considered professionals, they must be willing to hold themselves to a higher standard. They must do their job well, be loyal to their insurer, respectful to their colleagues and put their clients' needs above their own self-interest. The true professional is a person who performs with integrity and competence the obligations associated with his or her job.

As professionals, property-casualty insurance agents must pay particular attention to their motivation for the actions they take, the advice they provide and the continuing service they perform. As stated earlier, the easiest solution may not necessarily be the most appropriate in light of the ethical considerations involved.

In the following chapters, we will concentrate on how professional agents can pursue ethical relationships with their insurers, policyowners, communities and industry. We will look at ways in which agents can make rational, ethical choices that can benefit both themselves as individuals and society as a whole.

▪▪▪▪▪ Ethical Issue Number One

UNAUTHORIZED KNOWLEDGE

Martin owns the Bethany Insurance Agency, a property-casualty agency in Pennsylvania. He was recently appointed by the Penn/General Group and the Penn/Auto Insurance Company, responsible for both commercial and personal line products. Martin was excited at the appointment because the insurer was very well-known and respected throughout Martin's marketing area. He saw the new relationship as a major advantage for his agency and did not want to jeopardize this new beginning.

Martin was also very excited about his upcoming college reunion in Illinois. He had not been to a reunion party for many years. He was looking forward to seeing his college buddies—especially his longtime friend, Randell. They had known each other since grade school, and Martin had even been the best man at Randell's wedding. Throughout their lives, they had competed for grades, trophies and professional status. However, since Martin moved to Pennsylvania, they had had little contact other than an occasional telephone call and holiday card. Now Martin planned to impress Randell (a successful architect) with the success of his insurance agency and the appointment with Penn/General.

Over dinner, Martin and Randell discussed their lives, families and favorite hobby—collecting and restoring old sports cars. Martin's current project was a 1965 Mustang convertible; Randell's was a 1974 Barracuda.

"You know," Randell said, "I had the car 80 percent completed and was driving on Broadway to pick up some new weather stripping, when I got hit from the rear. I wasn't hurt but I cracked the fender and the steering was knocked out of line. You should have seen the kid who hit me . . . scared to death hitting a 'Cuda and all."

Randall continued, "There was no question about who was at fault and, fortunately, the kid was insured. Anyway, when the kid's insurance adjuster called, he asked about the damage. Well, you know, that car was involved in an accident before I got it and I had replaced the bumper, but this guy didn't ask about previous damage so I told him that the bumper was also damaged in the accident. The replacement I originally bought was only $50 or so. I had the old bumper in the garage and the ding was in about the right place. So, the adjuster comes out, looks, doesn't say a thing and writes a check for $450 on the spot, including $200 for the bumper! What a guy!"

Martin noticed his friend was quite pleased with himself and the extra money he got from the company and asked, "So, who was the kid insured by?"

"Some company called the Penn/Auto. Must be pretty small, I've never heard of them before. You know of them, Martin?"

"Certainly do. They're big in Pennsylvania, but they mostly write commercial insurance. You know, factories, office buildings and like that. So . . . what did you say to the adjuster after he gave you the check?"

"What could I say, but 'thank you,' and head straight for the bank. Ordered new carpet for the 'Cuda with the extra cash. You know these insurance companies. They have so much money, they won't miss a mere $450. You think I should write them a thank-you note, or what?"

Your Comments Please

1. What are Martin's ethical issues in this case? What are Martin's options and obligations?

   _____
   _____
   _____
   _____
   _____

2. What would you do in this situation?

   _____
   _____
   _____
   _____
   _____

3. Would you change your position if the amount were $600? $1,000? $2,500? Why?

   _____
   _____
   _____
   _____
   _____

2
Responsibilities to the Insurer

One potential source of ethical conflict for insurance agents can be the lack of understanding of the contractual relationship they have with their companies. Understandably, an individual new to the insurance business, or one joining a new company or agency, will be concerned with the day-to-day matters that affect insurance sales—matters such as territories, commissions, products, training, support, service, underwriting practices, premium rates, and competition from other insurance agents and companies—and may have little time to contemplate the other duties and responsibilities he or she has accepted by joining the agency or company. In this chapter, we examine the ethical responsibilities an agent owes to his or her insurer.

■ ■ ■ ■ ■

■ THE CONCEPT OF AGENCY

Insurance is a contractual arrangement by which one party, the insurer, assumes all or part of a risk that would otherwise fall upon another party, the insured. An insurance company is usually formed as a corporation and it appoints representatives to act on its behalf. Because of certain statutes, an insurer appoints licensed insurance agents to represent its interest to the insurance buying public. Insurance agents, acting for the insurer, establish insurance contracts with the general public on behalf of the insurer.

The relationship between an insurance agent and his or her company is governed by the concept of *agency*. "Agency" is a legal term that describes the relationship between two parties, in which one party—the *principal*—has authorized the second party—the *agent*—to perform certain legally binding acts on the principal's behalf. A principal may authorize an agent to do anything the principal might have done for its own benefit. In most agency relationships (including that of an insurance company and its agents), these acts involve making contracts between the principal and outside parties. In carrying out these duties, the agent, in effect, "becomes" the principal and assumes its identity when performing the authorized acts. When an agent acts within the scope of his or her authority, the law takes the position that the actions of the agent are also those of the principal.

An agency is created when both parties agree that the agent will act on the principal's behalf for the accomplishment of some purpose. The principal or the agent (or both) may be a corporation, a partnership or an individual. Insurance agents may be appointed for any legal purpose, such as binding insurance contracts, collecting premiums from insureds or adjusting insured losses.

Let's pause for a moment to consider the implications of an agency relationship.

- An agent is an agent of the principal, not the third party with whom he or she deals.

- An agent has the power to bind a principal to a legal contract and its obligations.

- By law, the acts of an agent, within the scope of his or her authority, are the acts of the principal.

Thus, you can see the significance of an agent's role to his or her company. By appointing others to act for it, the company is entrusting its agents to carry out its business and meet its goals and objectives.

How is an agent charged with this responsibility? Agency can be created by three methods: (1) appointment; (2) estoppel; or (3) ratification.

Agency by Appointment

When a principal and an agent wish to enter into an agreement to create, modify or terminate contractual relations with a third party, they usually enter into an explicit contract for that purpose. In most cases, the contract will be in writing, but it is not always legally necessary to do so. However, in the property-casualty insurance business, a written document called the *agency contract* usually designates the parties and outlines the specific authority of the agent who has been *appointed* to act for the principal, or the insurer.

Agency by Estoppel

In some cases, an agency relationship may be created even without an express agency contract. When the principal allows someone holding himself or herself out to be an agent of the principal to act in such a way as to lead an innocent third party to believe that that person (the "agent") has the power to act on behalf of the insurer, the insurer may be *estopped* (or barred) from denying that such an agency exists. If the third party reasonably believes that the agent was acting on behalf of the insurer, an *agency by estoppel* has been created.

In order for agency by estoppel to exist, three things are required. First, the principal must act in some way to create the appearance that an agency relationship exists. Second, an innocent third party must have been misled by the principal's actions and made to believe that an agency relationship exists. Finally, the innocent third party may be injured by acting in the belief that an agency relationship exists.

Let's look at an example. Assume that Silver Sands Insurance Company cancels its agency contract with the Farewell Insurance Agency, but fails to retrieve its applications and other policy forms from the agency. During the next several days, Farewell sells Silver Sands' homeowners policies to six new clients. These clients were unaware that Farewell's agency contract with Silver Sands had been canceled. Silver Sands' action in leaving its applications and policy forms in Farewell's office misled the clients into believing that Farewell was an agent of Silver Sands. As a result, the policies issued to the six new clients will be valid against Silver Sands, just as if the original agency contract remained in place. In other words, Silver Sands is "estopped" from denying that Farewell is its agent and, in fact, must honor the contracts. However, the new clients may be unable to renew their homeowners policies or may be asked to move to a new agent at renewal.

Agency by Ratification

Agency may also be created by ratification. *Ratification* occurs when a person holds himself or herself out as having authority to act for the principal when, in fact, he or she has no such authority. Ratification may either extend the previously granted powers of an agent or create an agency where none previously existed. Basically, ratification results when the principal later formally sanctions the previously unauthorized actions of an agent.

For example, assume that Bill Booker, who has no connection with Panda Insurance Company, convinces Metro Taxi Service that he is an agent of Panda Insurance Company and negotiates a liability contract with Metro Taxi Service that will generate $5 million in annual premium for Panda Insurance. Bill takes the agreement to Panda Insurance Company's home office and the regional vice president for the casualty division agrees to write the business, thus ratifying Bill's action and creating an agency for at least that one contract. It is also possible that Panda Insurance has created an agency by estoppel for future transactions, unless it formally notifies Bill Booker and Metro Taxi Service that no further agency relationship exists.

■ AUTHORITY OF AN AGENT

The essence of an agency relationship is *power*. Before an individual can act as an agent and establish contracts between the principal and third parties, he or she must have the power to do so. In the case of an insurer and an agent, this power is granted through an agency contract, which is how an insurer appoints an individual to act on its behalf.

The concept of *authority* is related to the concept of power. Though the two words are often used interchangeably, their definitions are distinct. The agency contract gives the agent the *power* to act on behalf of the principal and, at the same time, describes the actions the agent is *authorized* to take. Technically, only the authorized acts of an agent can bind a principal; practically and legally, however, an agent's authority can be quite broad. For example, an agent is given the power to sell and service an insurer's policies, but is authorized to do so only within a certain geographical area. One of the important implications of an agency relationship, and occasionally a source of conflict, is that an agent has the power to take actions he or she may not be authorized to take.

By most definitions there are three types of agent authority: *express, implied* and *apparent.*

Express Authority

Express authority is the authority the principal explicitly gives to the agent, either orally or in writing. Usually specifically granted in the agency contract, express authority spells out the actions the agent can, and cannot, perform for the principal. For example, through the agency contract, a property-casualty insurance agent is given the express authority to solicit applications for homeowners and auto insurance and collect the initial premiums for those policies.

Implied Authority

Implied authority is derived from express authority and is necessary to accomplish the purpose of the agency. Implied authority is that authority which the principal intends for the agent to have but does not expressly give. It includes those acts that are incidental to the accomplishment of the expressly authorized acts. For instance, when an insurer has expressly authorized an agent to solicit an application for insurance and accept premium payments, it also implicitly authorizes the agent to issue an insurance binder or, in some cases, a policy that is binding on the insurer.

Apparent Authority

Generally speaking, the powers of the agent are limited to express and implied powers. For innocent third parties, who do not know the extent of these express and implied powers, the authority of the agent is sometimes extended by yet another set of powers, known as *apparent authority.* Apparent authority arises when a principal permits an agent to perform acts that have been neither expressly nor implicitly authorized. In effect, the principal creates the "appearance" of authority. If a third party in good faith relies upon the principal's intentional or negligent permissiveness in regard to the agent's acts, the principal will be bound by the acts of the agent because the agent possessed apparent authority.

However, as explained earlier, the apparent authority of an agent must be derived from the actions of a principal. For example, if an agent's agreement with an insurer authorizes him or her to solicit applications only within a specified geographical area, but the company accepts an application and issues a policy outside that area, the apparent authority of the agent to operate outside that area has been established (or ratified) by the insurer. Statements or actions of an agent alone are not sufficient to create apparent authority.

Limitations on Authority

Rarely is an agent's authority to act for a principal unlimited. In most agency relationships, an agent's activity is restricted to some extent. For example, while an insurance agent is authorized to solicit applications and may even bind coverage in some cases, the final decision to accept or reject the risk lies with the insurance company's underwriter.

In addition, an insurance agent cannot modify a contract or waive exclusions, unless that authority is granted under the terms of his or her agency contract.

An insurance agent also cannot adjust premium rates. This act is reserved for the company. Typically, the limits to an agent's authority are spelled out in the agency contract, and it is within those limits that an agent must act. To step beyond is to invite problems.

This brief overview of the concept of agency was included to provide the basis for understanding the contractual relationship an insurance agent has with his or her company. Obviously, the ethical significance is that an agent must, first and foremost, serve the insurer, live up to the contract and operate within the scope of his or her authority. But actually, an agent's duty to the insurer goes far beyond the wording of the contract. By entering into this contractual relationship, an agent has also entered into a *fiduciary relationship*.

■ THE AGENT AS A FIDUCIARY

A *fiduciary* is an individual whose position and responsibilities involve a high degree of trust and confidence. Trustees, guardians and executors, by virtue of their responsibilities, are fiduciaries. So are insurance agents. An insurer places a great deal of trust and confidence in its agents; consequently, an agent must exercise a correspondingly high degree of fairness and good faith, and must act in the best interests of the insurer.

Through his or her appointment, an insurance agent is generally given the power and express authority to act for the insurer by:

1. soliciting applications for coverage;

2. describing coverages and policies to prospects and applicants and explaining how such policies can be purchased;

3. collecting premiums (or in some cases, only initial premiums with subsequent billings being issued and sent by the insurance company); and

4. providing service to prospects and the insurer's policyholders.

Thus, while the provisions of the agency contract tell agents *what* acts they are authorized to make, *how* they go about those tasks is usually left to their own judgment and discretion. However, make no mistake—both an agent's actions and judgments are held to fiduciary standards.

Serving in a fiduciary capacity demands high ethical standards and performance. In fact, those who depend on fiduciaries exact of them a higher standard of conduct than is required in the usual course of events. For example, assume a customer at a grocery store is mistakenly given more change than is owed. Ethically, the customer should return the difference—that would be the right thing to do. However, other than the motive or desire to do what's right, there's nothing else compelling the customer to give back the additional money. By comparison, a fiduciary acts in accordance with ethical standards, not only because it's the right thing to do, but because he or she *must*. That is the essence of a fiduciary role.

So, let's look beyond what an agent is expressly authorized to do and examine the ethics of the fiduciary relationship he or she has with the insurer.

Loyalty to the Principal

The primary ethical responsibility an agent owes to the insurer is *loyalty*. This means that he or she must, at all times, act in the insurer's best interest in every matter involving the insurer's business. Thus, by extension, an agent cannot act for himself or herself, if personal objectives run counter to the insurer's interest.

For instance, in many agency relationships, unless the agent is specifically authorized to do so, he or she cannot represent competing principals. It is quite common, however, for independent insurance agents and brokers to represent several insurers with the full knowledge and consent of the other insurers.

An agent is also charged with conforming to the limits of his or her authority and staying within the guidelines of the agency contract. For example, except for the compensation specified in the agency agreement, an agent cannot earn additional profits from the agency relationship by using the principal's name for personal gain or by investing premiums in the stock market until they must be remitted to the company.

Reasonable Care

An agent has a duty to carry out his or her actions with the utmost *care* and *skill*. The fiduciary relationship is a special relationship of trust and confidence that requires a high degree of care and integrity. As the insurer's authorized agent, the agent represents the company to the public and must act accordingly. In some cases, this means the agent must refer the business to others who are more qualified if the agent does not have the skills to handle it.

Full Disclosure

An agent is obligated to fully disclose all information that may affect the insurer and its ability to conduct business. Practically speaking, *full disclosure* is most significant during the application and claims handling processes. An agent must complete all applications and claims forms as accurately and completely as possible. Failure to do so could lead the insurer to follow a course of action it would not otherwise take (such as issuing a policy to an applicant whose bad driving record had been concealed). Thus, it is the agent's or broker's responsibility to see that the answers to questions on the application are recorded fully and accurately. Anything less than full disclosure may prompt the insurer to act in a way that is contrary to its own interests.

Provide Information and Follow-up

An agent has the obligation to act promptly in all matters regarding the insurer's business, but most significant is the responsibility to transmit completed applications and notice of bound coverages as quickly as possible. The insurer cannot begin the process of underwriting and issuing insurance until it has received an application and, unless the applicant has been given a *binder*, he or she remains at risk until a policy is issued. On the other hand, if an applicant is given a binder at the time of application, the insurer is obligated to provide coverage, until and unless the application is formally rejected. In either event, a delay by the agent in turning over an application may place the applicant or the insurer in jeopardy.

Handling of Premiums

In most states, an insured may be billed for insurance coverage in one of two ways: (1) the insurance company may invoice the insured and the premium is sent directly to the company; or (2) the insurance agent or broker may invoice the insured and the premium is remitted to the agent or broker. Most agents and brokers are authorized to collect initial premiums from applicants when the application for insurance is completed. Some are also authorized to invoice and collect renewal premiums on behalf of the insurer.

Premiums collected by agents or brokers are usually held in a *Premium Fund Trust Account (PFTA)* for up to 90 days (or some other date specified by the agency contract) before they are remitted (less any commission due the agent or broker) to the insurer. Only the commission due the agent or broker may be removed from the PFTA for the agent's or broker's use.

By law, payment to an agent is payment to the insurer. The agent has the fiduciary duty to account for all funds he or she receives in connection with the insurer's business, and to turn these funds over promptly. Even if there is no illegal intent, it is unethical to delay or withhold premium payments. In many states, it is illegal to combine premium monies with personal funds and rarely would it be ethical to do so, whether or not such a specific law exists.

Avoiding Conflicts of Interest

Insurance is a contract of "utmost good faith" between an insurance company and an insured. The parties involved in the contract must deal with one another honestly and fairly. As representatives of insurance companies by virtue of the agency contract, agents are affected by the agreement they make or have made with their clients and/or company or companies. Consequently, the agent is obligated to do the best job possible, with honesty, integrity and technical competency. If the agent makes promises or representations that induce the client to act on inaccurate representations, the agent may be liable either to the client or the insurer for any damages that result.

Captive Agents

An insurance agent who has signed an exclusive contract with one insurance company or a group of companies is called a *captive agent*. The insurer maintains ownership and control of any account generated by the captive agent. In return for a salary or a salary plus commission, the captive agent owes a singular loyalty to the exclusive insurer; it would be unethical for a captive agent to represent two insurance companies selling the same or similar policies.

In addition, a captive agent has the ethical obligation to inform his or her company about any other related service he or she provides and for which payment is received. An agent who does part-time tax preparation and filing, for example, or who serves as a consultant to a local business should inform his or her company of this activity. The insurer can then determine if there is a conflict of interest.

Independent Agents

Independent agents, who typically represent a number of companies, also face a conflict of interest when they attempt to serve their clients while being contracted to a number of insurers. *Independent agents* belong to a system of insurance sales, marketing, distribution and service in which the agents are independent businesspeople who own the renewals and are compensated by commission (or fees) as opposed to being salaried only or salaried/commissioned employees of an insurance company. If the independent agent and an insurer terminate their contractual relationship, the agent has the right to renew the policies with a different insurer so long as the policyholder approves the change.

Conflicts may arise because independent agents usually must place a specified amount of business with each insurer. For example, assume an agent must write ten new homeowners policies with a particular insurer each month. To assure that this quota is met, the agent may be tempted to only offer new clients a quotation from that company rather than "shopping" the policy with several companies. In some cases, the client might be better served by another insurance company that offers more or different coverage.

Although the agent represents the insurer, he or she must also attempt to serve each client by providing the best coverage at the most competitive premium. The agent may feel torn between serving the insurance company and the client because generally an agent cannot act as an agent for both parties in a transaction. Conflicts can be avoided if the independent agent follows the guidelines that apply to *dual-agency*:

- The agent represents the insurance company when insurance is being applied for and when it is in the process of being underwritten, in record-keeping, in claims settlement or other insurer-related activities.

- The agent represents his or her client only during the process of helping the client select the insurance plan best suited to the client's needs. It is up to the agent to see that the policy is written properly so that coverage applies where needed and as intended.

Careful Solicitation

An agent has the ethical duty to protect the insurer's interests by soliciting business that appears to be good and profitable for the insurer. Although at some point every agent will submit an application that is rejected or will write business that quickly lapses, the obligation to exercise reasonable care in soliciting quality business is obvious.

At the same time, once an agent has taken an application, he or she has the duty to submit it, even if it appears that the applicant may be a poor or uninsurable risk. For example, an agent may have some misgivings about whether the applicant is being completely truthful about his or her driving record. If the applicant seems edgy or even angry when questioned about previous losses, the agent may be reluctant to submit the application to the company. However, it is his or her duty to do so. Whether or not an individual is issued coverage is a decision for the insurer's underwriters.

Competitive Integrity

The insurance industry is a highly competitive one. For an agent, there exists ample opportunity to conduct business inappropriately at the expense of a competitor. Misrepresentation or defamation of a competitor's character reflects negatively on the entire industry. As a duty to his or her insurer and to the industry itself, an agent must resist this temptation. Ethically an agent should acknowledge the worth of other agents and their policies, and compete only on the basis of the value of the products and service he or she can provide.

■ DUTIES OF THE PRINCIPAL TO THE AGENT

The relationship between the agent and the principal is not one-sided: the principal also owes certain duties to the agent. A rule of agency law is that the principal is responsible for all acts of agents when they are acting within the scope of their authority. This responsibility includes fraudulent acts, omissions and misrepresentations. Thus, the principal must carefully select honest, loyal and hardworking agents to protect itself from potential liability. In return, the principal compensates the agent for entering into the agency relationship.

Compensation

Both parties hope to gain from the agency relationship. The most important duty that the principal owes the agent is compensation, or payment, for the business the agent has given to the principal. This compensation usually is in the form of commissions that vary by line of insurance. For example, the agent may receive 15 percent commission on a homeowners policy but only 3 percent on a workers' compensation policy. The commission rate on renewal business may be the same or lower than on new business, depending on the company. Agents who receive lower renewal commissions, however, tend to move the business to a new insurer each year.

Employment

When the agency agreement is signed, the principal must specify a reasonable period of time during which the agent is expected to produce a certain amount of business. The agency agreement usually spells out the type of business, the amount of premium that must be generated, the amount of commission that will be paid for each line of business and the length of time the contract will remain in effect. If the agent fails to meet the terms of the contract, the principal may terminate the agreement, withhold compensation or reimbursement or, if the agent has realized personal profits in excess of those stipulated in the agency agreement, sue to recover the excess profits.

Indemnity

The principal is also obligated to reimburse the agent for any damages or expenses incurred in defending against claims that the agent may be held liable for in the course of fulfilling his or her agency obligations. However, if the agent is guilty of breach of duty or lack of due care that harms the principal, the insurer may sue and recover monetary damages from the agent.

WHO IS AN AGENT OF THE INSURER?

Up to now our discussion has focused on the relationship between the insurer and the insurance agent. The preceding explanation of legal and ethical principles has been based on the assumption that the agent is someone who legally represents the insurer and has the authority to work on the insurer's behalf.

But do these same principles apply to agents who represent more than one insurer? And what is the relationship of an insurance broker to an insurer? Are brokers held to different standards? Let's take a look.

Is a Broker an Agent?

As explained in Chapter 1, unlike an agent who represents an insurance company, an insurance *broker* legally represents the insured. A broker acts as an independent contractor and does not have the authority to bind the insurer. (In some cases, brokers are also licensed as agents and they then have the authority to bind their companies as agents.) A broker may attempt to place business with more than one company and has no exclusive contract requiring that his or her business first be offered to a single company. A broker is paid commissions by the insurers where the business is placed. Legally, a broker obtains insurance for anyone who requests him or her to do so and represents the customer. For this reason, the insurance broker is an agent of the applicant.

An agent of one insurer may also have a broker's license and submit an occasional application to another insurer. This can happen when coverage is not offered by the first insurer but is available through the second insurer. A property-casualty insurance agent may represent the insurer for some purposes and the applicant for others.

There is an exception to the general rule that an insurance broker represents the client. This occurs when an insurer gives a policy to a broker for delivery to an insured. During the delivery process, the broker becomes the agent of the insurer. Should collection of a premium be involved, payment to the broker would be considered payment to the insurance company.

A Broker's Responsibilities to the Insurer

The insurance broker represents the buyer of insurance in most parts of the insurance transaction and, therefore, owes all of the duties of an agency relationship to the client. However, even though a broker technically represents the client, the ethical and fiduciary standards that apply to an agent also apply to a broker. For example, a broker has the duty to fully disclose all information he or she has regarding an application for insurance. A broker is also charged with carrying out his or her actions with utmost skill and care. A broker should seek quality business and provide prompt, exacting service. A broker must compete fairly and ethically, relying on his or her abilities, and not operate at the expense of other agents.

Actually, it makes little difference whether an individual represents one insurer or works with a number of insurers; the ethics and fiduciary standards are virtually identical.

■ SERVING THE INSURER SERVES THE CONSUMER

Perhaps the greatest source of ethical concern for many agents and brokers is the feeling that they are caught in the middle between two parties who have conflicting interests. On the one hand, an agent's primary responsibility is to serve the insurer. On the other hand, the agent also owes dedication, loyalty and service to the consumer.

As stated earlier, a person cannot act as an agent for both parties in a transaction. It is likely that such a situation would create a conflict of interest and some question of loyalty. How can an agent reconcile this conflict? Actually, it's quite simple. By acting in the best interests of the insurer, the agent best serves the consumer. This is the subject of our next chapter.

▪▪▪▪▪ Ethical Issue Number Two

"I'LL GLADLY PAY YOU TUESDAY..."

Robert started the Flatirons Agency on a shoestring, nurturing his clients and his contacts in the insurance industry. Celebrating his third year in business, Robert has built a solid base and represents five companies, including The United Insurers, for personal and commercial insurance. He has hired three full-time employees—two outside salespeople and one internal office employee. All three are licensed agents and have been promised commissions for any business they generate. June, the inside employee, has been charged with general office management, including the collection of premiums and payment of the bills for the office.

After five months on the job, June suspects that Robert has overextended the agency. He has leased cars for himself, his wife and the two salespeople. In addition, the salespeople have telephones in their cars and the agency picks up the entire tab for both business and personal calls. Robert has also used agency funds to purchase four season tickets for the major league baseball season. After checking the books, June realizes that the agency is generating some new business, but it is not retaining many renewals. Now Robert has asked that June book a one-week vacation for him and his wife to Mexico using the agency's credit card.

"Robert," said June, "I don't think we can pay for this right now. The notices just came in for the premiums on the JC Electrical and Harwood accounts. We need to pay The United and may not have enough money."

"No problem," Robert said as he started searching through his card file. "Call the bank. We can delay making the entire payment to The United for a month or so. Take $10,000 from the general agency account and take $5,000 from the Premium Fund Trust Account for premiums collected this month. Put the $15,000 in a 30-day CD and then roll it over for a second term. That should give us some breathing room and still pay for part of the trip."

"Also, don't pay the phone bill this month. Send a partial payment to The United Insurers. I've done it before and they don't squawk too loudly. And don't pay our auto insurance premiums this month. We write the policies out of this office; we can delay paying ourselves. I have two new large prospects pending and we should be back on track in a couple of months."

June followed Robert's instructions. However, the prospects did not materialize into accounts. June was then ordered to continue partial payments to all five insurance companies. Two months later, The United wrote the Flatirons Agency, demanding full payment for the written policies or they would be canceled for nonpayment of premium. United also indicated that it received a complaint from the Insurance Department indicating that premiums were not returned to two clients who had canceled their policies. The refunds were credited four months earlier and the accounts were reconciled at the home office. The United wanted a full explanation of what was happening.

Robert wrote the company, saying that he thought the return premium was paid and that he was enclosing a check for his past-due account. He asked June to write checks for the current month plus a partial payment for the past-due amount. He also asked that return premium checks be sent to the former clients, but didn't mention returning part of his commission to United for those accounts. Finally, Robert wanted to know when the CD was due and if the bill for his vacation had come yet.

Though uncomfortable with the requests, June wrote the checks and sent them to the consumers and United. Two weeks later, she started to receive telephone calls from the agency's current clients asking why they were receiving cancellation notices even though they paid the Flatirons Agency for their policies.

Your Comments Please

1. Has Robert violated his fiduciary responsibility to his clients? To The United? How?

2. What would you suggest to June, as a licensed agent with The United, when she first heard Robert's various schemes?

3. What is The United's responsibility to the Department of Insurance?

4. Can The United cancel the insurance policies for nonpayment?

5. What business advice would you give Robert and June?

3
Responsibilities to the Consumer

Some people feel that the greatest single obligation an insurance agent has is to his or her policyowners. Yet, if an agent is an agent of the insurer, how can this be? Isn't an agent's primary loyalty to his or her insurer? How can an insurance agent serve the best interests of both insurer and policyowner? Isn't this dual agency prohibited? The answer lies in knowing that these interests are not really in conflict. By promoting the concepts insurers stand for and by selling the appropriate products in the appropriate situations—in a competent, professional manner—the agent meets the needs of both the insurer and the insured. In this chapter we discuss how agents can fulfill their ethical responsibilities to policyowners through properly evaluating prospects' needs, providing quality service to clients and adhering to the principles of risk management.

■ ■ ■ ■ ■

■ PROPERTY-CASUALTY INSURANCE COVERAGE

Property-casualty insurance is usually classified by several major lines of insurance: fire insurance and allied lines, marine insurance, casualty insurance, multiple-line insurance and fidelity and surety bonds. *Property insurance*, such as fire or homeowners policies, covers the loss or damage to real estate or personal property from fire, lightning or other covered perils. *Marine insurance* (also called transportation insurance) covers goods in transit against pure risks related to transportation, whether those goods are shipped over land (*inland marine*) or water (*ocean marine*).

A broad field of insurance called *casualty insurance* encompasses almost everything not covered by fire or marine insurance: automobile insurance, general liability, burglary and theft, workers' compensation, glass coverage and other miscellaneous lines.

The agent may also sell *multiple-line* or package policies that combine property and liability coverages. Finally, an agent may sell *fidelity* and *surety bonds* that provide the insured with protection against losses caused by the dishonest or fraudulent acts of employees or that provide monetary compensation in the case of a bonded person's inability to perform certain acts, such as the completion of the construction of a building.

■ PROPERTY-CASUALTY INSURANCE MARKETING SYSTEMS

Property and casualty insurance is marketed by independent agents, exclusive or captive agents, and brokers. Exclusive agents sometimes offer insurance from their insurer at a lower cost, due to lower commissions and reduced expenses resulting from centralization of underwriting, policy issuance and claims processing in the direct-writing system. Independent agents and brokers offer insurance consumers the most options, because they work with multiple insurers. The agents have an wider choice of coverages, prices and services for their policyholders. Historically, independent agents have been the predominant producers in the property-casualty field.

Independent (American) Agency System

As briefly mentioned in Chapter 2, many agents belong to a marketing system known as the *Independent (American) Agency System* (sometimes called the "Big I"). The *Independent Insurance Agents of America (IIAA)* has helped consumers become familiar with the "Big I" through advertisements that tout the value of the independent agent as the "more than one company agent." The independent agent may have his or her own office, working alone, or may be in a partnership with other agents working from that office. The independent agent may represent *any number of insurance companies* under contractual agreement and is compensated on a commission or fee basis for the business produced. In other words, these agents are *not* employed by the insurance companies they represent. They are independent businesspeople who represent several insurance companies, pay all their own agency expenses and make all decisions about how their agency operates.

As we've seen, independent agents legally represent the insurance company (or companies), but as a practical matter they also represent the insurance consumer. Agents operating under this system have considerable bargaining strength with the insurers they represent because they may write policies with whichever company offers the most appropriate coverage for the consumer. Because the property and casualty business is highly competitive, insurers are often willing to negotiate rates and commissions to obtain favorable business.

Consumers who purchase insurance through independent agents are considered by both agents and insurers to be the *agent's* customers rather than those of the insurer, and the insurance company does not generally deal directly with the insured.

Exclusive Agents

The *exclusive agency system* is prominent among large property-casualty insurers. *Exclusive* or *captive agents* represent *one insurance company* or *group of companies only*. These agents are paid a salary, commission or a combination of both. Under restrictions imposed by the insurer, the insured is considered to be the *company's* client rather than the agent's. Companies using captive agents own and control the account, policy records and renewals. If the agency relationship or employment of a captive agent terminates, the agent loses all rights and interest in the renewal business and related commissions.

Direct Writers

A *direct writer* is an insurance company that sells its policies through employees or agents who represent it exclusively. These agents usually receive a salary, or a salary plus commission for the business they produce. Some insurers, such as specialty fire insurance companies that emphasize loss prevention in insuring large, well-established industrial and institutional properties, negotiate their contracts primarily through salaried representatives in direct contact with executives of the business being insured. More commonly, however, policies are solicited and sold through the mail. A direct writer maintains complete control and ownership of its policies and renewals.

■ AN AGENT'S DUTIES AND RESPONSIBILITIES

Agents in the property-casualty field may be one of two types: (1) *general agents* who have authority to bind the companies they represent; or (2) *limited agents* who have reduced authority, based on more limited agency contracts. Usually, limited agents cannot bind coverage or issue policies. As stated, brokers cannot bind coverage or issue policies because they do not represent insurance companies.

As representatives of insurance companies through *agency contracts*, agents may be granted wide authority to inspect risks, to immediately bind an insurer by oral or written agreement, to issue various types of contracts, to collect premiums due, to settle some claims and so on. Consequently, the agent is obligated to do the best job possible for the insurer and the client. If the agent makes improper promises or representations that induce the client to act on those representations, the agent may be held liable to either the client or the insurer for any damages that result.

The range of quality of insurance agents is immense—some merely sell insurance; others act as advisers as well as motivators. It costs an individual no more in premium to buy coverage from a superior agent than it does to buy from an inferior one. However, it may actually "cost" insurance clients less in the long run to deal with reputable agents because such agents can help clients develop a risk management program and implement a plan to get the most for their insurance dollar.

Evaluating, Selling and Servicing

Before an individual becomes a policyowner, he or she is a prospect. The transition from prospect to policyowner, and ultimately from policyowner to client, comes about when an agent follows two basic rules: *sell to needs* and *service the sale*. In doing so, the agent will also live up to the ethical duties he or she has to policyowners.

An insurance agent has one principal reason for calling on a prospect: to offer a product or service that will benefit the prospect in some way. The property-casualty agent offers policies that provide *indemnification for losses*, an important benefit to society that permits individuals, families and businesses to be restored to a former financial position after a loss occurs. An agent must sell the kinds of policies that will best fit the prospect's needs and in amounts he or she can afford to pay. No one profits—not the insurer, not the agent and especially not the policyowner—if an individual is coerced or misled into buying too much insurance or purchasing coverage that doesn't suit specific needs.

Fortunately, most agents recognize that selling to fit needs is the best approach to the products and services they represent and wisely follow this path. They know that specific types of insurance policies are designed to meet specific needs, and matching policy to client need produces the maximum effect, to the benefit of the policyowner. They also know that needs selling involves problem analysis, action planning, product recommendation and plan implementation. This requires two important commitments on the agent's part:

1. a commitment to the knowledge and skills necessary to carry out those tasks; and

2. a commitment to educating the prospect or client about the products and plans that may be implemented on the agent's recommendation.

Commitment to Knowledge and Skills

The relationship between the professional insurance agent and the policyowner is usually built on the policyowner's trust in the agent's knowledge and skills. The policyowner must rely on the agent to provide informed options and trust that the recommendations for insurance are in the client's best interest.

The professional agent thus has an obligation to ensure that this trust is justified. This means an agent has the ethical responsibility to:

- Obtain the necessary knowledge and skills to evaluate and service the insurance needs of clients. Indeed, the term "professional" implies knowledge and skill. If the agent feels that he or she is not properly trained to perform the needed service, another professional should be called in to assist. For example, an agent untrained in loss prevention might enlist any number of loss prevention experts, such as safety engineers, occupational safety and health specialists or product liability underwriters.

- Keep his or her base of knowledge and skills current. To this end, the agent must be committed to a program of continuing education. He or she must also stay informed of the latest developments affecting a client's interests. In recent years, there has been an increasing trend toward insurance professionalism. Agents should be competent professionals with a high degree of technical knowledge in a particular area of insurance and who also place the needs of their clients above the their own.

Commitment to Educating the Prospect/Client

Client trust must be earned, nurtured and constantly reinforced. The agent who remembers this basic rule is the agent who communicates to his or her client the reasons *why* a particular insurance policy or program is being recommended and *how* it will serve. Individuals who understand what a particular insurance plan or policy will do for them are more likely to buy, more likely to be satisfied with their insurance and more likely to renew their policies. This communication and education continues long after the particular policy or program is sold and becomes part of the overall insurance program designed for that client. As noted earlier, the professional agent has established his or her client's insurance program based on needs. These needs should be reviewed annually, supported by explanation and communication of the programs put in place to meet those needs.

■ SELLING TO NEEDS

In securing coverage for your client, your main responsibility as an agent is to act reasonably under the circumstances. This means that you must also adhere to your ethical responsibilities to the insurer and see that the prospect completes the application accurately and completely.

At this point, your *primary* responsibility is to the insurer since you are acting as its agent during the application process. The agent is responsible for obtaining full and accurate information necessary for analyzing the risk and the hazards and exposures involved in order to determine the prospect's needs accurately. Remember that the insurer is relying upon you for full disclosure of all pertinent information regarding the applicant.

The agent should explain the services he or she and/or the insurer will provide for the client, such as those involving safety programs, claims handling and so forth, to assure that the policy is written properly so that coverage applies where needed and as intended. Therefore, before completing an application for insurance, the agent should study the risk by physically inspecting the prospect's property and gathering full and accurate information about the risk. For example, this may involve taking photographs, making diagrams of buildings or listing scheduled personal property. He or she should then complete an application, a key source of information for rating the policy. The application and other pertinent information should then be forwarded to the insurance company as soon as possible.

The Importance of the Application to the Applicant

The agent also has an ethical responsibility to educate his or her prospective client so that he or she fully understands the nature of the application process: why the information is required, how it will be evaluated, the need for accuracy and honesty in answering all questions and the meaning of insurance terms included in the contract, such as "coinsurance," "claims made vs. occurrence policy forms," "care, custody and control" and "subrogation."

All of the information submitted on an insurance application has a direct bearing on whether the policy will be issued as requested, whether the application will be rejected or whether another policy will be offered by the insurer. An agent who knowingly or unknowingly fails to provide all the pertinent information about a prospect is not serving anyone's best interest.

Consider, for example, a situation in which an agent does not disclose that the applicant for a homeowners policy is a retired animal trainer who keeps a declawed tiger as a pet. The agent reasons that if this information were revealed the company would decline to issue the policy, leaving the prospect uninsured. Believing that it would be in the prospect's best interest to have the insurance, the agent completes the application without noting the applicant's pet. The agent explains to the prospect that omitting this "detail" will keep the premium down and the applicant gratefully signs the application. Coverage is issued as a standard homeowners policy.

But, what happens if, nine months later, a neighbor is attacked and injured by the tiger? It's quite likely that the insurer will contest or deny the claim, citing concealment. Rather than receiving protection under the policy, the homeowner is likely to receive a cancellation notice. What benefit did this policy provide? What kind of service did the agent render?

This example illustrates why precision and accuracy in completing the application are in the best interests of both the insurer and the prospective insured. It is vital that an agent understands this and explains the need for full disclosure to a prospective insured.

Issuing Binders

An agent who has been given binding authority may immediately bind the insurer on the risk. A *binder* is a written or oral acknowledgment that immediate coverage is temporarily in effect pending issuance of the policy. It has the full force and effect of the policy.

The binder should contain a time limit, the name of the insurer, the amount of insurance, the perils insured against, the type of insurance, a list of exclusions and so on. A copy of the binder should be sent to the insurance company immediately so there is no misunderstanding by either the insurer or the insured as to when coverage takes effect.

Explaining the Underwriting Process

Another ethical responsibility you owe your applicant is to briefly explain the underwriting process that the application will undergo. Insurers are in business to make a reasonable profit and underwriting is important because the class of risk the underwriter selects affects the ratio of claims paid to premiums collected. The major function of the underwriter is to select risks that will fall into a "normal range" of expected losses. If the losses selected fall above the normal range, the rates charged will be inadequate to cover claims. If the losses fall below the normal range, the Insurance Department may request that the insurance company revise its rates to avoid excessive premiums.

Although many insurance policies are issued on the basis of the application alone, others require additional information. No prospect should ever be surprised that he or she could be subjected to further underwriting. Therefore, the explanation of the underwriting process should include a description of the checks and balances that apply to underwriting a risk, such as how information gathered about the risk will be used to analyze, underwrite and rate the risk.

Field Underwriting

Every agent or broker needs to engage in some type of *field underwriting*, the process of screening out unacceptable risks. There is no point in submitting risks that obviously will be rejected by the insurer, because that wastes your time and that of your client. And, if the agent submits poor risks consistently that *are* accepted, his or her book of business with the insurers will suffer and the agent might jeopardize his or her relationship with them.

Some agents have the authority to issue policies for the risks they have underwritten. Copies of the application, binder of insurance and the policy are sent to the insurer. Even though a policy has been issued, the insurance company underwriter may send a notice of cancellation if he or she finds that the risk was poorly underwritten and does not meet company guidelines. If the underwriter decides to remain on the risk, he or she may require repairs, such as exterior paint, a new roof or debris removal, to continue coverage.

Agents can build a higher quality book of business and establish sound relationships with insurers by engaging in responsible field underwriting. This involves analyzing risks and exposures, taking steps to avoid or reduce risks, considering loss control efforts and submitting risks to the proper markets. However, the agent cannot perform all the needed underwriting services. The insurer is in a better position to check financial information and driving records of applicants, for example.

Company Underwriting and Rating

As stated earlier, when a risk is submitted to an insurance company underwriter, he or she makes a final decision whether to accept or reject the risk. In order to do this, a number of factors must be weighed. One of the most basic and important factors is whether the applicant has an *insurable interest* in the property to be insured. Insurable interest exists only when a person or an institution can suffer a financial loss if that property is damaged or destroyed. There must be a greater interest in preserving the property than destroying it. If there is not an insurable interest, buying insurance is similar to gambling, and the contract of insurance becomes unenforceable in the courts.

Once insurable interest has been established, company underwriters consider a number of factors when evaluating a risk. They examine the nature of the risk, what hazards are present, what outside factors might affect the risk and what past losses have occurred. These factors determine whether the risk is acceptable and also help to determine the final premium.

The *premium* is the total cost for the insurance coverage (or limit of liability) purchased, and is calculated from the *rate*—the amount of dollars or cents per particular amount of insurance the risk generates. *Base rates* have been developed for various risks and these rates are multiplied by an *exposure base* (i.e., amount of insurance, payroll, sales, area). Thus, if the base rate for fire insurance is 20 cents per $100 of insurance, the gross premium for a building insured for $100,000 would be $200 ([$100,000 ÷ 100 = $1,000] × .20).

Some risks are *class rated*, which means that the loss history of a class of risks having similar characteristics (i.e., male drivers age 25, jointed masonry buildings in a particular urban area, etc.) was used to develop the rate. Class rates may readily be applied to most dwelling and some mercantile establishments because of their similarity of construction and use. Underwriters usually have the option of applying rating modifications, based on the loss history or special characteristics of a risk. For example, risks may be *experience rated*, which means that the insured's actual past loss experience plays a major role in the development of the rate. When an underwriter is particularly familiar with a certain type of risk, he or she may use *judgment rates*, based largely on the underwriter's knowledge and experience.

Unlike homeowners risks which are class rated, *commercial risks*—whether mercantile, manufacturing or mining—and *institutional risks* generally do not share similar characteristics. Therefore, *specific rates* are applied to business establishments and public buildings by using *schedules* to determine the relative risk involved. The individual risk is inspected and measured against a theoretical average, receiving credits for factors that exceed the average and surcharges for factors that fall below the average. Various items that contribute to risk of loss from fire or other perils are weighed by an established standard to determine a rate of premium. These items include the building's

- type of construction;
- location;
- occupancy or use;
- amount and types of fire protection; and
- exposure or hazards from surrounding buildings.

For example, it is logical that occupancy as a woodworking enterprise in an unprotected frame (wood) building would represent a different degree of risk than occupancy as a metalworking factory in a noncombustible (metal or gypsum) building and would, therefore, generate a different rate.

Complying with the Fair Credit Reporting Act

An insurance company may hire a consumer reporting agency to obtain personal information about an applicant for underwriting purposes before a policy is issued. The *Fair Credit Reporting Act* is a federal law that helps to ensure confidential, fair and accurate reporting of information about consumers—including applicants for insurance. The Act stipulates that consumer reports may be furnished by consumer reporting agencies only for certain purposes, which include the underwriting of insurance. Applicants for insurance must be advised that such reports may be obtained and, within certain guidelines, consumers may demand to know what information an investigative agency has on file about them and to whom such reports have been made. Consumers also have the right to insist that disputed information be reinvestigated and corrections be made and sent to anyone who received a consumer report about them.

The Inspection Report. Insurance companies usually require an inspection or an appraisal of the property to be insured. An appraisal is an estimate or opinion of value. Value in real estate terminology, is the present worth of future benefits arising from the ownership of real property. Most insurers use professional appraisers to determine the value of the property by calculating the replacement cost of the property based on the construction cost at current prices of similar structures. Insurers require insureds to maintain insurance equal to a specified percentage of the replacement cost of the insured property. The agent should explain that the *coinsurance* clause is required in fairness to other policyowners who would otherwise be paying more than their share of premiums and in order for the insurer to have adequate premiums to pay for losses.

The Credit Report. Most commercial insurers order a credit report to determine the applicant's ability to pay premiums and to determine whether he or she may be a poor credit risk. Again, the purpose of this report should be explained when the agent asks the applicant to sign the application for insurance.

■ PROVIDING SERVICE TO CLIENTS

Selling to needs is only part of what an agent must do to meet the ethical responsibilities he or she owes to a policyowner. *Service*—during and after the sale—is just as important.

The term "service" means many things and no two people would define all that it entails in precisely the same manner. However, for purposes of this discussion, we will cover the elements of service in the context of ethical selling and professional responsibilities.

In all instances, the agent is responsible for:

- maintaining accurate records about his or her clients (for example, current addresses, types of vehicles, occupation, etc.);

- maintaining complete and accurate written records of all business transactions (i.e., pending applications, binders and binder charges and premium accounting);

- keeping informed about changes in markets, new coverages and product availability that might expand coverage for a client or provide potential for additional sales to prospects or clients;

- assisting clients with their service needs, such as name changes on policies, changes in mode of premium payment, etc.;

- assisting clients in filing claims by reviewing claims procedures and providing the insured with a loss report form and by later following up on the status of open claims; and

- contacting clients before renewal dates to: (1) review their existing policies and their values and limits in light of any changes in hazards and exposures that may have occurred; and (2) then recommend suitable changes in coverage as necessary.

Confidentiality

In the course of qualifying a risk, completing an application, analyzing financial needs or determining appropriate coverages, insurance agents are privy to a client's personal and financial information. Ethics require that the agent respect the sensitive nature of this information and keep it confidential. Personal information about a client should never be released without proper approval from the client.

Full Disclosure to the Applicant

As has been emphasized throughout this text, insurance agents have a duty to fully disclose to the insurer all material facts concerning an applicant or policyowner, or situations involving either, in order to assist the insurer in making any decision regarding a risk. At the same time an agent has the ethical responsibility of full disclosure to a prospect or client.

In this context, *disclosure* means informing the prospect or client of all facts involving a specific policy or plan, so an informed decision can be made. This helps meet other goals, too, by helping the client:

- select the most appropriate policy to meet his or her needs;

- understand the basic features of property and casualty insurance; and

- evaluate the relative costs of similar plans offered by a competitor.

Keeping the Applicant Informed

The underwriting process for an insurance application can be time-consuming. Most insurance companies strive to complete the process within a 21-day period, assuming that there are no delays. Delays can occur whenever an underwriter needs additional information from the applicant and relays that request through the agent, or whenever a counteroffer, a different policy or a different rate is proposed to the applicant, again through the agent.

It is an agent's duty to help ensure that there are no unnecessary delays in the underwriting process. This does not mean that you have to rush from your office to the nearest post office to mail an application. It does mean, however, checking the application for accuracy and giving careful thought to the information provided and the coverages offered before the application is submitted. Many underwriting delays occur simply because the application is not complete or is not clear.

Applications, binders, pictures, building diagrams and other pertinent underwriting information should be submitted to the insurer as soon as possible. The time frame will vary, of course, depending on the plan of insurance and the complexity of the risk. An agent must take these factors into account in order to move in an efficient manner. If it appears that the underwriting process may take longer than anticipated, the agent should notify the applicant of the delay.

Delivering the Policy

After the policy is issued and prior to policy delivery, the agent should check to be certain that the coverages, limits, forms, endorsements and so on are contained in the policy as requested. Although most homeowners and personal automobile policies are forwarded to the insured in the mail, the most successful agents will often deliver commercial policies in person. By delivering the policy in person, the agent will have the opportunity to review with the client the contract, its provisions and special features. The agent should carefully explain coinsurance, deductible provisions, exclusions (especially on all risk policies) and any other important information in the policies being delivered. Explaining the policy and showing how it meets the policyholder's specific needs, reinforces the sale and helps to avoid misunderstandings. It also serves to build trust and confidence on the part of the client in the agent's abilities and desire to be of genuine service.

Most policies are issued as applied for. On the other hand, some policies will be surcharged or rejected because the risk does not meet the insurance company's underwriting guidelines. In other words, the risk does not fall within a normal range of expected losses. When this happens, the agent has two responsibilities:

1. *He or she should personally review the rating or rejection.* Was there an unfavorable inspection or credit report that resulted in higher rates? Was something overlooked or not made known to the underwriter? Should additional information be submitted? Is the rating or rejection proper? Should the application be reconsidered? In any event, the agent should have as much information as possible and be able to explain the higher premium or rejection to the applicant.

2. *Assuming the rating or rejection was valid, the agent has the responsibility to notify the applicant promptly.* To withhold this information in an effort to prevent the applicant from seeking insurance elsewhere is a breach of ethics and could actually harm the applicant and his or her family.

■ RISK MANAGEMENT

In addition to providing sales and service, the agent or broker should also provide some risk management for the prospect or client. *Risk management* is the process of making and carrying out decisions that will protect assets and income against accidental or unintended loss. This involves utilizing available resources to identify, measure, control and treat risks. Insurance is often either the sole or partial solution to risk management problems.

Many large corporations employ risk managers, but risk management is not restricted to large companies. Its theory and methods apply as well to the small business owner, the individual and the family. Consequently, agents, brokers, loss control representatives, claims adjusters and underwriters serve as risk managers in various degrees in the course of their daily work.

Rules of Risk Management

We often consciously and unconsciously make risk management decisions in our daily lives, e.g., when we attempt to manage our time, plan a career or institute our insurance programs. Even when people gamble they may consider and apply basic risk management methods.

There are two general, practical rules of risk management:

1. The size of the potential loss must relate favorably to the resources of the one who must bear the loss; and

2. The possible benefits of taking a risk must be reasonably related to the possible costs.

In other words, we should not risk more than we can afford to lose; we should consider the odds and avoid risking a great amount for little potential gain.

Application of Basic Rules

To apply these two basic risk management rules, the agent or broker must learn certain facts about the risk. The process of risk management can be time-consuming because the agent must have a full understanding of the insured's assets, liabilities, income and activities. This may mean the completion of risk questionnaires or checklists, insurance surveys, personal inspections, financial statements and/or flowcharts. All these aides help the agent to avoid overlooking some loss exposures that might go uninsured or uncovered by some other risk management technique.

The agent or broker must take the following actions to learn certain facts about the risk.

- The loss exposures and hazards need to be identified and measured. This may involve discovering all the potential *pure risks* (risks that offer no chance for gain if they occur, such as the chance of death or disability, of physical damage to property or of fraud or criminal violence). For each loss, the agent then must estimate the potential *frequency* (the number of times a particular type of loss has occured in the past is a measure of the probability of future loss) and *the severity* (the size or financial impact of a loss that determines the seriousness of those losses that occur). The evaluation and measurement process is a vital part of risk management because it ranks potential loss exposures by seriousness and points out those that require immediate attention. For example, a fire might (1) damage a building and its contents; (2) cause an employee's death; (3) cause damage to neighboring property; and/or (4) make it necessary to move or close the business, at least temporarily.

- The amount of money that will be available to meet the potential loss must be determined. The insured may be financially able to bear a large loss or, if not, he or she may need to transfer most of the risk to another party through a hold-harmless agreement or insurance.

- The benefits and costs of available alternative methods of dealing with the risk in certain situations must be considered. As mentioned, insurance is often the solution; however, the ethical agent will consider other factors, such as loss prevention or self-insurance, that also may be the necessary and proper action to take under the circumstances.

Risk Management Techniques

Although property-casualty agents are in business to sell insurance, there are other methods to deal with loss exposures that agents might recommend to their clients. The major risk management techniques are:

- avoidance;

- transfer (other than insurance);

- retention;

- loss control; and

- insurance.

Regardless of the size of the risk, most risk management programs consist of more than one technique. For example, an individual might select homeowners coverage (insurance) with a deductible (a form of retention) and install smoke detectors and a burglar alarm (loss control measures). Or a person might choose to take public transportation to work rather than buying an automobile and having to insure it (avoidance). But an insured who drives to work could elect to garage the car rather than parking on the street (loss prevention), thus complementing his or her auto insurance and lowering the premium. In this case, the selection of additional risk management techniques is not an alternative to insurance but an addition to it.

Avoidance

Although it is not always possible to do so, one of the simplest ways to handle risk is to *avoid* it. A corporation can avoid potential losses by refusing to manufacture a particular product; an individual can avoid certain potential liability losses by refusing to own a vicious dog or by declining to build a swimming pool.

As a general rule, a risk should be avoided when its potential for loss is greater than the possible gain involved. Avoiding risk may involve changes in company practices and methods of doing business. However, sometimes risks cannot be avoided when they are essential to the business or to a person's lifestyle.

Transfer Other Than Insurance

Loss exposures may be *transferred to another party* before or after a loss. There are many methods available for transferring risk, such as though the use of subcontractors, hold-harmless agreements, surety bonds, warranties and so forth. One of the simplest methods of risk transfer is *incorporation*. When an individual invests in a business, he or she incurs the risk that the business may fail, leaving debts for which the individual may be liable and that exceed his or her original investment. The corporation entity is a legal device to which this risk may be transferred; the risk of the shareholders or investors in the corporation is limited to the amount each paid for his or her shares. This, of course, is a method of dealing with *speculative risk,* which involves the chance of both loss and gain.

Retention

Many agents recommend that an insured *retain* all or part of a risk by means of a deductible. In return for a reduced rate, the insured assumes losses below a certain amount. For example, automobile comprehensive and collision deductibles, whereby the insured bears the small losses and the insurer pays the larger ones, are means of partially retaining risk.

Loss Control

Unlike avoidance, *loss control* does not totally eliminate the possibility of loss; it simply strives to reduce the chance or amount of loss. When loss can be predicted somewhat accurately, it often can be controlled through *loss prevention* (lowering the frequency or probability of loss), *loss reduction* (lowering the severity of the losses that occur) or a combination of the two. For example, some bodily injury losses can be prevented with adequate safety training and property losses can be reduced with the installation of a sprinkler system.

Insurance

In most cases, the agent will recommend insurance as the cornerstone of any risk management program. *Insurance* transfers the risk from the insured to the insurer through the insurance mechanism of spreading risk among a large number of exposures. In many instances, insurance is the most economical method to finance losses. The agent can assist the consumer by explaining the available coverages, rates and insurance services, including inspections, claim service and legal assistance.

Choosing the Best Methods

When the agent is acting as a risk manager, he or she will choose the best method or combination of methods for handling risk. Making the best decisions involve considering:

- the reasonable amount of risk to be assumed or retained, and determining which loss can be prevented, reduced, avoided or transferred, based on the client's financial condition; and

- the client's philosophy, attitudes and desires with respect to risk and the ways of handling it.

Risk management also involves a well-planned program for future reassessments of the plan—identifying the client's changes in loss exposures, ability to bear losses, financial picture and insurance needs. For example, if the agent initially chooses insurance as the primary risk management technique for a pharmaceutical company, he or she will: (1) recommend insurance coverages best suited to each loss exposure; (2) suggest a reasonable deductible that meets both the insured's financial abilities and the insurer's guidelines; (3) negotiate the rates and rating plans that recognize loss control efforts; and (4) set up a system to monitor claims reports and payments that affect renewal premiums. The agent might also recommend that the company delay the introduction of a controversial new drug to avoid potential lawsuits. Finally, the agent may suggest surety contracts as loss financing transfers. Under the terms of a surety agreement, or *bond,* one party becomes answerable to a third party for the acts or neglect of a second party.

Implementing the Decision

Once the risk management techniques have been selected, the risk management program must be implemented and communicated to all concerned parties. The agent or broker should clearly identify the possible financial costs of losses to the property itself (or loss of use of that property) and the liability exposures that may arise from contractual and tort liability claims for damages to others or their property, along with methods of treating these risks. If the individual or corporation is firmly committed to risk management and trusts the agent's expertise, the suggested recommendations should be implemented.

Monitoring the Results

The final step in the risk management process is monitoring the results of the selected program to determine whether it is working. As stated earlier, this is an ongoing process that permits the agent or risk manager to make changes as needed. For example, a loss frequency problem may necessitate the inclusion of a higher deductible or a reevaluation of the loss control methods selected.

■ BUILDING A TRADITION

When an insurance agent participates in the risk management process for a client, he or she assumes important responsibilities. The client looks to the agent as a professional who can provide sound advice and, when necessary, can work with other experts in applying the principles of risk management. And, when insurance protection is necessary for transferring risk, the agent can be expected to propose a practical and thorough insurance plan that provides proper coverages in the correct amounts to offer adequate protection at the most reasonable cost.

In most cases, an insurance agent needs only common sense to avoid an unethical situation with a policyowner. However, there are some specialized areas where the agent's ethical conduct is specifically detailed. For example, an agent has both a fiduciary and professional responsibility to insureds and applicants for insurance. Failure to secure the insurance needed by the client could be a breach of trust that could leave someone without needed protection when a loss occurs.

After the policy is issued and an applicant becomes a policyowner and client, service becomes more than your ethical responsibility—service now forms the base upon which you and your client establish a lasting relationship. All policyowners should receive periodic reviews to ensure that their insurance programs are in step with their plans and objectives. Service after the sale is more than a responsibility; it is part of a property-casualty insurance industry tradition. Agents through the years have helped build that tradition and your future success as an agent depends upon you continuing that tradition.

■■■■■ Ethical Issue Number Three

"MIS-APP"

Andrew Martinez enjoyed teaching "Homeowners Contract and Law Review," a continuing education class. He heard interesting comments and "war stories" from the participants, and Andy knew many of the attendees personally. His current class had over 30 students from four agencies, Andrew entertains questions during the breaks, lunch and after the eight-hour class session was completed.

Liz and Bill Miller were seasoned agents and had been in other classes that Andy taught. As partners, the Millers were very pleased with their relationships with their clients and the companies they represented. Over the years, the Millers' reputation for fairness and honesty was unsurpassed.

As the class broke for lunch, Liz approached Andy. "Andy, can you join Bill and me for lunch? Our treat. We have a dilemma that is bothering us, and you may be able to give us some direction." Andy agreed and met Liz and Bill for lunch.

"We have a problem," Bill explained. "We have clients, the Hannock family, who have been through some very hard times. We insure their cars and now they want us to insure the house. The wife has been laid-off. Tim's mother has been very ill and their oldest son is having major problems in school. To top it all, they suffered a loss from that huge hailstorm last year, Tim had his golf clubs stolen and, the other day, someone vandalized their garage, breaking windows and spray-painting the door. They haven't reported it to the insurance company yet."

"Tim's current homeowners insurance is with another agent who represents Atlas Insurance, a company we also represent," Liz continued. "We know that Tim's hurting and will probably be canceled by the Atlas based on claims frequency. We're thinking of advising them not to make the claim. Now, they are asking that we write their homeowners insurance through our agency without indicating the hail loss and the vandalism. If we do report the losses, Bill and I know that the insurance will cost them twice as much as they are paying now, if they can find coverage! And we don't have a "Fair Plan" for homeowners in this state, do we, Andy? What do we do? I really feel terrible for them."

"Unfortunately, Liz, there's no Fair Plan here," Andy replied. "How big were the claims and how long have these folks been insured with their current company?"

Bill sipped his coffee and thought for a moment. "The golf clubs were about $700 and the hail cost the company about $4,000. I think the damage to the garage will run about $500. The Hannocks have been our clients for about five years now without one auto claim. And other than having the clubs stolen because the car doors weren't locked, the claims were not his fault. It doesn't seem fair to penalize him for a mistake like that."

"Although we don't currently write the Hannocks' homeowners insurance, they have technically 'reported' their homeowners claims to us," Liz continued. "We understand our obligations to the company. But we also feel that, well, we owe something to the Hannocks for being good customers. And they have become close friends over the years. Can you give us some direction, Andy? And, if we end up giving the Hannocks bad advice, what will the Insurance Department say?"

"You have one heck of a problem." Andy took a breath and was about to answer when the waitress delivered lunch.

Your Comments Please

1. What are the ethical issues facing the Millers?

2. What are the Millers' expressed and implied responsibilities to the company? To the Hannocks?

3. If you were Andrew Martinez, how would you advise the Millers?

4. If the Millers did not report the vandalism loss, would this be considered a violation of your state laws?

4
Responsibilities to the General Public

As stated in Chapter 2, agents and brokers, like many other professionals, have a fiduciary responsibility toward those persons they represent in an insurance transaction. This means that the agent's or broker's relationship to an insured is based on trust and confidence. Insureds trust the agent or broker to serve their needs in the best manner possible; they put their trust in being adequately protected against future losses into the hands of a professional, who is entrusted with this public duty. As a result, the insurance professional has a great degree of control over the public's attitude toward insurance. This is because the agent or broker often initiates contact with a prospect, determines a prospect's need for insurance, recommends and implements an appropriate plan and continues a long-term relationship with after-sale service.

Because the agent or broker has significant contact with the public and is a primary source of insurance information, public perceptions of the insurance industry can be severely damaged by unethical agents or brokers. As noted in Chapter 1, the professional insurance agent has two ethical responsibilities to the public: (1) to inform the public about insurance with the highest level of professional integrity; and (2) to strive for an equally high level of professionalism in all public contacts in order to create and maintain a strong positive image of the industry.

This chapter discusses those responsibilities.

■ THE NEED FOR INSURANCE

Imagine a world without insurance. Individuals involved in automobile accidents would have no way of recovering the cost of repairing their cars, paying for damage to property or receiving reimbursement for injuries. Businesses or homes destroyed by fire, hurricanes or floods might never be rebuilt since few people could afford to repair the damage or purchase a new building or home.

In addition to lost wages, workers injured on the job and unable to work would have no medical assistance to help them.

Property and casualty insurance plays a major role in the lives of most people in the United States. It is vital to the well-being of most Americans, providing a sense of security for individuals, businesses, community organizations and government units. Considering how important insurance is and how it benefits peoples' lives, insurance professionals sometimes wonder why it is that most insurance buyers do not take the time to read their policies and to understand insurance coverages.

Many consumers feel that insurance is one area in which a wrong purchase is easy to make. The terminology is confusing and the conditions and exclusions seem complicated. It may not always seem that the agent is working in the consumers' best interest. Moreover, if consumers are not thoroughly familiar with the type of coverage they need *before* they purchase insurance, they will only find out they purchased the wrong kind or wrong amount of insurance *after* a loss. What good is a policy that provides unnecessary coverage or does not live up to its promised benefits?

Insureds trust their agent or broker to serve their needs in the best manner possible. Producers can live up to this trust by respecting insurance laws and regulations, committing themselves to continuing education and adhering to a personal and professional code of ethics.

Insurance Laws and Regulations

Today there is joint federal and state supervision of the insurance industry, with the federal government retaining control in matters that are, or should be, uniform across state lines. For example, the federal government has jurisdiction in matters concerning employee relations, fair labor standards and other areas where all companies (including insurance companies) are subject to federal law. Also, the federal government conducts insurance programs in areas where commercial insurers are unable or unwilling to provide insurance, such as federal flood insurance, FAIR plans, federal crime insurance and federal crop insurance.

All other regulation is handled at the state level. State insurance departments, divisions or boards operate under the direction of a commissioner, a director, or a superintendent of insurance, who may be elected or appointed. Duties and operations of the various state departments of insurance include the following:

- issuing rules and regulations;

- licensing insurers, agents and brokers;

- suggesting laws to their legislators;

- examining insurance companies' financial operations;

- approving policy forms and insurance rates; and

- overseeing advertising and marketing practices.

Although insurance companies are subject to strict government regulation, many consumer groups are advocating even stricter controls over the ways in which insurers are permitted to do business. It should be noted, however, that as a matter of public policy, the law tends to favor the insuring public in cases where insurers have acted outside of their authority or outside the legal requirements set forth by the state. For example, the director or commissioner of insurance has the authority to revoke or suspend any license or certificate of authority that he or she issues to companies, agents or brokers.

The most obvious reason for taking this action against an insurance company would be the insurer's failure to limit the amount of new business it writes to the amount of its policyowners' surplus. In general terms, *policyowners' surplus* is the difference between a company's assets and liabilities. In property-casualty insurance, the insurer can safely write $2 of net new premiums for each $1 of policyowners' surplus in order to offset any substantial underwriting or investment losses. In addition, adequate policyowners' surplus is required to offset any deficiency in *loss reserves*, the estimated liability for unpaid insurance claims or losses that have occurred as of any given value date.

An agent or broker may lose his or her license by engaging in misleading or unethical marketing practices. Because many consumers are uninformed about insurance, it is possible for unscrupulous agents to take advantage of individuals by inducing them to buy policies that are unnecessary or that duplicate existing coverage. To combat this unethical behavior, professional insurance agents must offer the public an honest and fair explanation of the policies and services that they represent. They should clearly understand all federal and state rules, regulations and laws governing insurance and have the desire to perform their insurance duties in compliance with these restrictions. The Insurance Code in the state or states in which they are licensed sets forth the statutes designed to uphold the insurance professional's fiduciary position.

In addition, agents must learn as much as possible about the nature of various contracts on the market, be informed about new insurance trends and stay abreast of every aspect of insurance that would affect the insureds entrusted to their care. Agents must clearly explain policy features and benefits without misleading or misrepresenting any aspect. Furthermore, professional insurance agents must be ready to back up these promises with solid performance—and encourage other agents to do the same.

Continuing Education

Licensing is required of individuals working in insurance sales to help ensure that only competent and trustworthy individuals will be in a position to represent an insurance company. However, an insurance professional's education should not end with the successful completion of the licensing examination. Many states now require a licensee to continue his or her insurance education with accredited insurance coursework after passing the licensing exam. Courses are offered by various professional organizations and most major insurance companies offer specialized training courses for their employees and often for their agents or brokers.

Accredited classes are also available through other organizations. In 1904, Dr. S.S. Huebner, an instructor at the Wharton School of Finance and Commerce at the University of Pennsylvania, created the first collegiate educational program in insurance. Today, a number of junior colleges, colleges and universities have full curricula in insurance. In addition, many universities offer a master's or doctoral degree in insurance and/or risk management.

Many agents, brokers and others working in the insurance industry pursue additional advancement through certification offered by specific insurance societies. The first and oldest of these societies, the Association of Insurance Societies and Institutes of America (now known as the *Insurance Institute of America*), was founded in 1909 to ensure professionalism among insurance practitioners by stressing knowledge, skills and codes of ethics.

In 1941, as a result of a conference of a number of professional societies, a national college, the *American Institute for Property and Liability Underwriters*, was created with the power to issue professional designations in insurance. One such designation, the *Chartered Property and Casualty Underwriter (CPCU)*, is awarded to individuals who pass a series of ten complex written examinations covering a wide range of subjects, including insurance laws and procedures, risk management techniques and general business topics. In addition to rigorous coursework and national examinations, CPCUs are held to high moral and ethical standards.

The Insurance Institute of American and the American Institute for Chartered Property Casualty Underwriters offer a number of other designations, including the following:

- *Associate in Claims (AIC)*—a designation for experienced claims adjustors, claims personnel and individuals who deal with property and liability claims;

- *Associate in Risk Management (ARM)*—a designation that offers training in the identification and evaluation of loss exposures and loss control for those responsible for controlling and financing risks of losses suffered by their own company or for individual clients;

- *Associate in Underwriting (AU)*—a designation for those who deal with the selection, design and implementation of loss control programs and the underwriting of property and casualty risks; and

- *Associate in Management (AIM)*—a designation for middle management that concentrates on the strengths and weaknesses of management practices, human behavior and decision-making processes.

These (and a variety of other professional designations) can help individuals gain prestige and recognition within the insurance industry while demonstrating their commitment to professionalism.

Professional Code of Ethics

The public's trust and confidence may also be enhanced by an insurance agent's adherence to a code of ethics provided by any number of professional associations or organizations. In addition, many corporations have (1) implemented codes of ethics, which are formally articulated statements of corporate values, (2) sponsored training and educational programs in ethics and (3) installed internal judiciary bodies that hear cases of improprieties. When insurance professionals strive to live by these ethical guidelines, they strengthen the status and standing of all insurance professionals in the eyes of the public they are striving to serve.

Codes of ethics usually require that professionals keep pace with rapidly changing conditions and current issues in insurance regulation. They further require that professionals keep informed on those technical matters that are essential to the maintenance of professional competence. For example, the American Institute for Chartered Property Casualty Underwriters and The Society of Chartered Property and Casualty Underwriters share a *Code of Professional Ethics.* The Code emphasizes a high level of professional competence and adherence to lofty ethical standards as the most important characteristics of a true professional. The Independent Insurance Agents of America's Code of Ethics outlines the independent insurance agent's commitment to the public, to his or her companies and to fellow members of the IIAA. (These codes are reprinted in their entirety at the end of this text.)

At the 1994 annual meeting of the American Association of Managing General Agents, two executives speaking on behalf of the insurance industry indicated that agents and brokers will have to do business in ways that will enhance the public's perception of the insurance industry. The president of the National Association of Professional Insurance Agents, Charles Crowley, Jr., stressed that in order to prosper in the 21st century, agents will have to be committed to higher standards of quality, ethics and financial disclosure. Echoing that sentiment was Courtney Wood, president of the Independent Insurance Agents of America, who said, "Continuing education is a win-win situation."*

ISSUES FACING INSURERS

Property-casualty insurers have faced a number of complex ethical issues over the past several years, including whether unisex rating is viable for automobile insurance rating, whether antirebating laws discourage competition and are harmful to consumers, whether redlining should be permitted in some cases and whether a Superfund reform bill is feasible. These issues are often hotly debated and, in view of the trend toward deregulation and greater price competition, it is likely that all insurance companies will have to come to terms with a number of complicated issues involving insurance regulation.

Unisex Rating for Auto Insurance

As part of its rate-making process, insurance companies use their past loss experience and industry statistics. For example, in addition to the insurer's own loss data, industry statistics on hurricanes, tornadoes, fires, crime rates, the cost of living and so forth are also used as part of the data to establish premium rates for a particular type of insurance. Actuaries in property-casualty insurance have also used *gender* in determining rates for automobile insurance premiums; they contend that men and women should pay different rates because their loss experiences are different. Based on its statistics, the insurance industry argues that

---

* Brian Cox, "Higher Standards Expected When Dealing With MGAs," *National Underwriter,* May 23, 1994, p. 2.

female drivers should pay less for their automobile coverage because they have fewer and less expensive claims than male drivers.

However, some consumer groups, such as the *National Organization for Women (NOW)*, see gender-based rating as discriminatory, arguing that under this system women (who generally live about eight years longer than men) will actually pay more for all forms of insurance over their lifetimes than men. They have proposed that *unisex rating*, which means that the pooled loss experience of both males and females is used to calculate the rates charged, be used for all types of insurance.

Unisex rating is now used in many group life and health insurance plans that are experience rated. NOW maintains that only objective actuarial data, such as miles driven, driving records, place of residence and so on, should determine the final premium for automobile insurance.

Rebating

The subject of rebating commissions elicits strong emotional responses, both pro and con. *Rebating* occurs if the buyer of an insurance policy receives any part of the agent's commission or anything of significant value as an inducement to purchase a policy. In some states, a company or person convicted of a rebating violation is guilty of a misdemeanor. Also, an agent or broker who is found guilty of rebating may not receive any commission for selling the policy associated with the rebate. If paid in error, such commission may be recovered by the insurance company. (However, it should be noted that insurance codes/regulations vary by state and some may permit small forms of inducement.)

The Argument Against Rebating

In most states, the practice of rebating is illegal and the following are defined as illegal inducements to buy:

- offering, paying or allowing any rebate or other inducement, not specified in the policy, or any special favor or advantage concerning the dividends or other benefits that will accrue, in order to place, negotiate or renew the policy;

- offering, selling or purchasing anything of value not specified in the policy; and

- offering, paying or allowing any rebate of any premium on any insurance policy or annuity contract.

The Argument for Rebating

Those in favor of abolishing all antirebate laws argue that these laws are protectionist legislation designed to preclude price competition among insurance agents. They point out that the insurance industry no longer needs the antitrust exemption of McCarran-Ferguson, and that the law should be repealed. Furthermore, many life agents use the argument that a form of rebating (called *negotiated commissions*) already exists in the property and liability area. [Note: This argument fails to consider that commercial insurers, who place great reliance on rating and advisory organizations and market forces, are able to accurately determine adequate premiums and adjust those premiums with almost surgical precision. It is far easier to negotiate commissions on commercial property and liability policies, where prices are highly volatile because of the cyclical nature of the business, than on personal lines, life or health policies.]

Regardless of your own feelings about the subject, some states, such as Florida and California, currently allow some rebating. In Florida, for example, rebating is allowed if the agent follows six specific rules.

1. The rebate has to be available to all insureds in the same actuarial class.

2. The rebate must be in accordance with a rebating schedule filed by the agent with the insurer issuing the policy to which the rebate applies.

3. The rebating schedule shall be uniformly applied so that all insureds who purchase the same policy through that agent for the same amount of insurance receive the same rebate percentage.

4. Rebates shall not be given to an insured who purchases a policy from an insurer that prohibits its agents from rebating commissions.

5. The rebate schedule is prominently displayed in public view at the agent's place of business and a free copy is available to insureds on request.

6. The age, sex, place of residence, race, nationality, ethnic origin, marital status, occupation or the location of the risk is not used in determining the percentage of the rebate or whether a rebate will be available.

Redlining

Many insurers argue that they need to control potential losses and that they should be permitted to limit coverage or even refuse to write homeowners coverage in areas where losses have been frequent or severe. However, under the provisions of the *Fair Housing Act*, a licensed individual or company may *not* refuse to provide homeowners or renters insurance solely on the basis of the geographical location of the insured's property. Rejecting coverage solely because of a risk's geographical location is known as *redlining*. The practice of redlining occurs when a company "draws a red line" (either actually or by implication) around a specific geographical location and refuses to insure properties located within its boundaries.

When coverage *is* issued in a redlined area, another pervasive form of discrimination takes place that involves charging higher premiums for comparable policies, charging higher rates for inferior policies and refusing to provide replacement cost coverage on the structure and contents of homes in minority neighborhoods. Some insurers and their agents justify their refusal to write coverage because the homes in these neighborhoods are too old or their value is too low. Before issuing a quote, insurers might require homeowners to give the agent the name of their mortgage lender to obtain further information about the risk or they might require an inspection of the premises before discussing the type and cost of policies available. Typically, the insurer will also require credit checks of minority applicants.

The U.S. Department of Housing and Urban Development (HUD) prosecutes insurance companies that intentionally engage in practices that have the intent and effect of denying, limiting or restricting homeowners insurance for people living in minority neighborhoods throughout the United States.

■ ISSUES FACING INSURANCE PRODUCERS

Insurance agents and brokers must work hard to succeed, and occasionally, in the pressure of competition, certain lines of unfair conduct are crossed. Though fortunately it is not a widespread problem, when an agent or broker does behave unethically, it not only can damage the reputation of the producer but, in the long run, the entire insurance industry. The issues that can present some ethical concerns for producers can be broadly classified into one of the following three areas:

1. skill and competence issues;

2. obligations associated with a commitment to—or lack of—professionalism; and

3. moral issues stemming from individual behavior.

Skill and Competence Issues

Many ethical problems agents face or create for themselves can be traced to a simple lack of *skill and competence.* For example, some agents feel that failure to identify prospects' needs and recommend appropriate products is a problem, as are agents who misrepresent their ability to provide competent service. Yet it is obvious that these problems would not exist if agents were knowledgeable and competent. A thoroughly trained, knowledgeable, competent agent would not fail to identify a prospect's needs nor would the agent have to misrepresent his or her insurance capabilities.

Skill and competence are prerequisites to selling insurance. These two qualities are the means by which an agent provides informed options and recommendations that are in the client's best interest. Thus, an agent has the ethical responsibility to:

- *Develop and maintain a high level of knowledge and skill through concentrated study and dedicated work.*

- *Acknowledge those cases or situations that are beyond his or her skill level.*

Commitment to Professionalism

A number of ethical issues can develop when an agent lacks a commitment to *professionalism.* For instance, disparaging the competition, failing to be objective with others in business dealings, not providing prompt, honest answers to clients's questions and failing to provide products and services of the highest quality in the eyes of the customers were problems the industry faces. However, agents who make a true commitment to professionalism will not be hampered by these conflicts. Professionalism requires an agent to:

- *Place the client's interest beyond one's own self-interest.* Professionals are loyal to their clients and are dedicated to protecting their clients' welfare. This means they remain independent and objective in their judgment and evaluations and recommend plans or policies that most benefit the client. When a policyowner asks for help or advice, the agent is quick to follow up, embracing client service as an important responsibility.

- *Be dedicated to his or her industry and supportive of all its member companies and representatives.* A true professional aligns himself or herself with colleagues and competitors alike, knowing that all represent similar products and services, and that all should share a commitment to the purpose and goals of these products and services.

- *Offer quality plans and represent quality companies.* A professional agent represents only those companies with solid financial standings; he or she accurately informs prospects and clients of an insurer's financial position as part of the sales process.

Moral Issues

Finally, insurance professionals face at least two problems when they are competing with other agents or brokers who are less principled than they should be. These two problems are: (1) agents who offer false or misleading representations of products or services; and (2) the temptation that exists between opportunities for financial gain (or other personal benefits) and the proper performance of one's ethical responsibilities.

While many questionable practices can be condemned as being immoral or unethical, perhaps the root of the problem is a lack of knowledge or understanding on the agent's part. The agent who misrepresents a policy may not recognize that what he or she is doing is unethical. After all, if a prospect needs insurance, does it matter how it is sold? The answer, of course, is "Yes!" If a sale can't be made with honesty, fairness and objectivity, it must not be made at all. If there is an opportunity for personal gain, but it comes at the expense of another, it must be ignored. Thus, the ethical agent:

- *Learns very early the difference between right and wrong in business and sales practices and acts accordingly.* He or she develops high ethical standards through training with experienced professionals and association with industry groups.

- *Consistently adheres to his or her values and maintains this integrity throughout his or her sales career.* The ethical agent resists conflicts of interest—real or perceived—in all business dealings. Ethics emphasize the interests of clients and company over one's own interests.

- *Willingly assumes the obligation to perform his or her duties in a way that reflects the highest degree of dignity on the industry and best serves the interests of the client or prospect.* Occasionally, this means that the agent must put service above sales.

■ PUBLIC PERCEPTIONS OF THE INSURANCE INDUSTRY

There are two indisputable facts about insurance and the buying public: first, the average insurance buyer knows very little about insurance and therefore relies on the advice and recommendations of the insurance agent; and second, by the time a consumer discovers that a particular policy does not meet his or her needs or does not live up to the agent's promises, it may be too late to purchase another. The potential for deceptive advertising or promotion by companies and agents alike is significant and the consequences to the consumer can be quite grave.

Accordingly, all states have enacted laws prohibiting agents from engaging in unfair or deceptive acts or methods of competition with respect to selling and servicing insurance policies. The basis for many of these state statutes is the NAIC's model *Unfair Trade Practices Act,* which expressly cites false advertising as an unfair trade practice and prohibits it. In this context, the term "advertising" is quite broad. It includes print and radio material, descriptive literature, sales aids, slide shows, prepared group talks, brochures, sales illustrations, policy illustrations, television ads—in short, almost any kind of communication or presentation used to promote the sale of an insurance policy.

As you'll learn in more detail in Chapter 5, the purpose of the NAIC model act is to establish guidelines to ensure that insurance companies and their agents promote their products properly and accurately, without exaggerating the benefits or minimizing the drawbacks. Generally speaking, the burden of complying with state insurance advertising laws rests on the insurance companies, since most advertisements or promotional pieces, regardless of the writer or presenter, are considered the responsibility of the insurer whose policies are being advertised. In practice, most of the advertising and sales literature an agent uses is prepared by the insurer under the careful eye of its legal staff. Thus, for an agent, the ethical issue is not the material itself, but *how the material is used*—and the deceptive sales presentation that may result.

What constitutes a deceptive sale? Any presentation that gives a prospect or client the wrong impression about any aspect of an insurance policy or plan is deceptive. Any presentation that does not provide complete disclosure to a prospect or client is deceptive. Any presentation that includes misleading or inconclusive product comparisons is deceptive. Even if the deception is unintentional, the agent has done the consumer a great disservice.

Deceptive sales presentations can be blatant—a comparison of a Homeowners 2 (broad form) coverage and a Homeowners 3 (special form) based only on premium rates is obviously misleading and incomplete. Yet deception does not have to be this apparent to be unethical. What about describing a homeowners policy as "all risk," but failing to mention that several perils (such as earth movement, neglect, intentional loss and so on) are not covered or that special limits of liability apply to certain types of property?

What of recommending a Commercial Package Policy (CPP) without explaining the ways in which the premium might be reduced through higher deductibles or loss control? What about selling only occurrence-form commercial general liability policies without explaining the advantages and disadvantages of both the occurrence and the claims-made forms? What of a sales presentation that focuses the prospect's attention on the protection that a commercial umbrella policy provides without mentioning that, if the policy contains an exclusion that is also present in an underlying contract, the firm has no coverage under either contract for the loss? While any of these ploys might help make the sale, they are all misleading and unethical.

The Agent's Role

As an insurance agent, you represent your insurer to the general public—your prospective insureds. Through your actions you help shape the public's perceptions. Thus, as we have said before, your primary ethical duty to the public and each prospective insured is to provide accurate information regarding insurance policies and benefits in a fair and unbiased manner. That information should be complete in every way, providing the prospect with the details of any policy deductibles, conditions, limitations, exclusions or requirements. For example, an audit of a prospect's or client's current insurance policies helps to determine if they are up to date and in proper order, provide the type of protection needed and provide the best protection in the most economical way.

Your ethical duties to the public and your prospects are quite demanding. In addition to the attributes that most consumers expect from their agents—skill, competence, professionalism and moral integrity—let's review other ways in which agents can help (or hinder) the public's perception of insurance and the insurance industry.

Communication

A prospect's lack of understanding of precisely what an insurance policy will and will not provide is usually the result of poor communication. Sometimes the source of this problem is that an agent attempts to sell a new product without fully understanding the policy's features and benefits.

Attempting to sell a new policy, or any policy for that matter, without adequate knowledge and training is unethical since it is an agent's responsibility to determine if and how a policy will fit the prospect's needs. Understanding how policies "work" will help the agent determine that needs fit and also help the agent compare them to those of the competition.

Complete and Honest Representation

It is an agent's duty to present each policy with complete honesty and objectivity. This means pointing out any limitations, exclusions or drawbacks the product may have, along with its features and benefits.

The insurance buyer can suffer because of a misunderstanding about a policy's terms and conditions. If a loss goes uncovered because the agent or broker did not fully understand the risk, the buyer suffers. When a buyer suffers, the industry suffers. The best solution is to fully understand the insurer's policies and forms and to also be aware of its underwriting, pricing and claims settlement practices. It is then simple to explain the policies and practices to the prospect. In all cases, a simple, straightforward explanation of the policy and how that policy will help fit the prospect's needs is always the proper ethical course.

ILL. 4.1 ■

> **NAIC Guidelines for Insurance Advertising**
>
> 1. All insurance advertisements must be truthful and not misleading in fact or implication. Words or phrases that are clear only through familiarity with insurance terminology cannot be used.
> 2. All information required to be disclosed (i.e., exceptions, limitations of benefits and exclusions from coverage) must be printed conspicuously next to the statements to which the information relates and displayed in such prominence that it is not minimized, confusing or misleading (in short, no fine print).
> 3. Deceptive words, phrases or illustrations may not be used to describe a policy, its benefits, the losses to be covered or premiums payable.
> 4. Testimonials must be genuine, represent the current opinion of the author, be applicable to the policy advertised and be accurately reproduced.
> 5. Disparaging remarks or statements about another insurer, agency or agent of another insurer, their products and services may not be used in any advertisement.
> 6. The identity of the insurer must be clear in all advertisements, as well as the name, address and phone number of the agent placing the advertisement.

Selling to Fit Needs

A prime violation of an agent's ethical duty to a prospect is deliberately "selling to fit the needs of the agent" rather than the needs of the prospect. The typical result is a prospect being sold insurance with the highest premium (and the greatest commission) instead of the proper coverage.

The answer to this problem can be found in the American Institute's *Code of Professional Ethics,* which is shared by both the American Institute and The Society of CPCU. (The Code is found in its entirety at the end of this text.) The Code's Rules of Professional Conduct (R3.1 and R3.2) clearly state the following:

> *"In the conduct of business or professional activities, a CPCU shall not engage in any act or omission of a dishonest, deceitful, or fraudulent nature. A CPCU shall not allow the pursuit of financial gain or other personal benefit to interfere with the exercise of sound professional judgment and skills."*

■■■■■ Ethical Issue Number Four

"ELEMENTARY, MY DEAR WATSON..."

Anne Watson dreamed of becoming a professional pilot for a major airline after she graduated from college. With her aeronautical degree in hand, her dream came true when she was hired as a crew member flying 727s for National West. Unfortunately, the career was short-lived when she developed high blood pressure and could no longer pass the physical. While searching for a new career, Anne was approached by Jim Carlson, the owner of the Carlson Agency, a large and well-known general commercial insurance agency in northern California. He was looking for an aviation insurance specialist. No insurance experience was required, but a thorough background in aviation was necessary. Anne jumped at the opportunity.

After one year on the job, Anne was doing quite well. She had gotten her blood pressure under control and, though she could not pilot commercially, she was able to fly her private plane to visit clients in California. Her client base consisted of private aircraft owners, flying clubs and schools, a few small airports and one regional airline. Rex Jackson (RJ to his friends) was one of her private aircraft clients who owned a couple of businesses, including a surveying firm.

One day RJ approached Anne with the following proposition. "Anne, my son and I own a surveying firm in Sacramento. He runs the operation and just bought a Cessna 206 to get to the job sites. He'll need it insured and I know you'll want the business."

Anne was excited. This was her first referral and she knew if she did well with this account, RJ would refer more business to her in the future.

"Sure, I want the business. Just the one aircraft, RJ? You guys aren't planning to start a fleet, are you?"

"Nah... but the business insurance comes due in a month or so. You want to quote on it, Anne? Know anything about surveying, blasting and theodolites?"

Anne had never heard the term "theodolites" before but felt that if insuring aircraft had been easy, writing a surveying firm shouldn't be too difficult. "Sure," Anne joked. "That's how someone with a lisp describes the view of Seattle at night, right?"

With telephone number in hand, she contacted RJ's son, Leon, the next morning and made an appointment for two days later. She then talked to Jim Carlson to get a handle on this prospect.

"No one has written a surveying firm in this office before, Anne," Jim said. "However, go to the library, learn the language, fill in all of the ACCORD forms and you should have no problem. By the way, I'm taking two weeks of vacation starting tomorrow. See you when I get back."

Anne and Leon met the next day and quickly established a working relationship. She took all the information on the Cessna and then started to complete every commercial application form she was able to locate in the office that might cover the surveying business. As they were talking, Leon sensed that they were missing something.

"Along with everything else, Anne, we need E&O coverage, too. I currently have a one-year tail, so we should have no problem with overlap."

Anne had never heard of most of the surveying equipment Leon had mentioned earlier and now had no idea what an "E&O" or "tails" were. But Anne was determined to show Jim, RJ and Leon how good she was.

"When does your policy expire, Leon?" Anne asked.

Leon replied, "In three weeks. I hope that's enough time for you, Anne. If it's a rush, we can write the Cessna now and wait on the rest of the package."

"No. I'll have the entire quote with a couple of days to spare. No problem."

Anne left for the office, feeling frustrated and bewildered. The new language baffled her, but Jim would not be around to discuss her concerns. She would do it on her own and prove her worth.

Your Comments Please

1. What are the ethical issues in this case?

2. What should have Anne done before she visited with Leon Jackson?

3. Assume the role of Anne Watson's supervisor and suggest how she should have handled this case.

5
Ethics and the Law

Two of the most important ethical questions that all insurance practitioners should ask themselves are: "How does an insurance professional come to *know* what is right as opposed to what is wrong in carrying out the business of insurance?" and "How can I *do* what is right once I understand what is right?" In other words, once an insurance professional understands and embraces a personal and professional code of ethics, he or she must also find ways to avoid the temptation to act in illegal, unethical or questionable practices that could provide short-term profit at the expense of compromising his or her integrity.

Those who wish to have an agent's code of ethical conduct precisely defined often find some pleasure in state insurance statutes that define both acceptable and unacceptable ethical conduct. The purpose of this chapter is to review and discuss the ethical standards mandated by most states. We will also cover the personal values that many people hold that cause them to aspire to a higher standard of behavior than the law requires.

■ ■ ■ ■ ■

■ HOW THE INSURANCE INDUSTRY IS REGULATED

An important characteristic of the insurance industry in the United States is that it is primarily regulated by the states rather than the federal government. This has been true throughout the history of insurance in the United States. The U.S. Supreme Court, in the case of *Paul v. Virginia* (1868) seemed to settle the question of state-versus-federal regulation when it decided that the insurance industry should remain regulated by each state.

The rights of states to regulate insurance remained relatively unchallenged until the U.S. Supreme Court case of *United States v. Southeastern Underwriters Association* (1944). In that case the Court reversed its earlier decision and ruled that insurance should, indeed, be regulated at the federal level, as are almost all other interstate trades.

The *Southeastern Underwriters* case threatened to throw the insurance industry into turmoil. In response, the U.S. Congress enacted Public Law 15, better known as the *McCarran-Ferguson Act*. This law, passed in 1945, reserves for the federal government the authority to regulate insurance in areas such as fair labor standards and antitrust matters. All other insurance regulation is reserved to the states. As such, the states carry the major burden of regulating insurance affairs, including the ethical conduct of agents licensed to conduct business within their borders. This regulation of ethical conduct is spelled out by what is termed in some states "marketing ethics."

Regulation of an insurance agent's ethical conduct is usually conducted through an insurance commissioner's or director's powers to oversee the marketing practices of both agents and insurance companies in that state. As discussed in Chapter 4, many of the regulations governing ethical conduct are derived from model legislation developed by the National Association of Insurance Commissioners (NAIC).

The Role of the NAIC

All state insurance commissioners, by whatever title they hold in their respective states, are voluntary members of the NAIC. The organization has standing committees and has worked regularly to examine various aspects of the insurance business and to recommend appropriate state insurance laws and regulations. Its recommendations and *model laws* are studied by its committees and discussed at semiannual meetings in an attempt to attain some uniformity of insurance regulation and practice among the various states.

The NAIC has four broad objectives:

1. to encourage uniformity in state insurance laws and regulations;

2. to assist insurance officials in administering these laws and regulations;

3. to help protect the interests of policyowners; and

4. to preserve state regulation of the insurance business.

To promote uniformity among the various states in insurance regulation, the NAIC formulates and drafts what is called "model legislation." This term includes representative bills or statutes presented to the individual state legislatures for consideration and passage, creating insurance law for that state.

The NAIC has worked diligently to create model legislation that promotes fair and ethical sales and marketing practices by agents and insurers alike. Its model "Unfair Trade Practices Act," which has been adopted by virtually every state, seeks to regulate insurance practices by defining and prohibiting unfair trade and business practices. As you will recall from Chapter 4, prohibited practices include misrepresentation, deception or false advertising, twisting, inequitable claim settlement and unfair discrimination. The act gives the state's insurance commissioner the power to investigate insurers and agents when any violation is suspected. Punishment for violations includes not only a fine, but possibly suspension or revocation of an insurance license as well.

■ CONSUMER PROTECTION

All states have laws that regulate the sales and marketing practices as well as the licensing of brokers and agents. If the agent is incompetent or dishonest, the state insurance commissioner has the authority to suspend or revoke the agent's or broker's license; this provides powerful control over the insurance producer's behavior.

Though state laws regulating sales and marketing practices by insurance agents vary, there is a great deal of uniformity in the principle and intent of these laws. All are designed to protect the interests of consumers by ensuring fair, reasoned and ethical conduct by an agent.

Let's take a look at some of the most significant of these laws that protect consumers against illegal practices.

Commingling Funds

As discussed in earlier chapters, agents and brokers by law are regarded as acting in a fiduciary capacity in their handling of premium funds. They must use utmost care in what they do with these funds. The agent or broker may not *commingle* or mix premiums collected for insureds with any other funds held for business or personal use. They must have the express consent of each insurer they represent to establish a Premium Fund Trust Account (PFTA) for funds held by them due the company. However, they do not have to maintain a separate PFTA for each company as long as the funds held for each company are reasonably ascertainable from the agent's or broker's records. The agent or broker is entitled only to commissions and earned on the PFTA until the funds are transferred (less commission) to the insurers.

Unauthorized Insurers

By law, only insurers that have been authorized or licensed by a state may issue policies in that state. Consequently, an agent must make sure that the insurers he or she represents are licensed to do business where solicitation is made. *State guaranty funds* operate in much the same way as the FDIC does for banks and other institutions. The funds provide a means for paying at least part of an insured's losses if his or her property-casualty insurer becomes insolvent and is unable to meet its obligations to its policyholders. The amount of reimbursement is subject to both a deductible and a limit of liability, depending on the state. Generally speaking, a state's guaranty fund only covers the liabilities of authorized insurers, so anyone purchasing policies from unauthorized or unlicensed companies would be at risk if those insurers could not meet their claims. Some states will hold the agent personally liable on any insurance contract he or she places for an unauthorized insurer.

Unfair Marketing Practices

As stated above, agents or brokers found guilty of an unfair marketing practice or unfair method of competition may be fined and have their license suspended. Whatever the case, the agent must cease and desist from continuing such practices. Repeated violations will likely result in license suspension or revocation.

Some of the more common unfair trade practices are:

1. *Misrepresentation and/or false advertising.* As we have stressed throughout this course, agents have an ethical duty to present their policies in a truthful and open manner. Any written or oral statement that does not accurately describe a policy's features, benefits or coverage is considered a misrepresentation, and states have enacted laws that penalize agents who engage in this practice. Misrepresentation or false advertising includes issuing, circulating or making false estimates, illustrations or statements about the provisions of a policy, its benefits or advantages or about the general condition of any insurer. It is also unlawful to make any misleading representation or comparison of companies or policies to insured persons to induce them to forfeit, change or surrender that insurance.

2. *Defamation.* Any false, maliciously critical or derogatory communication—written or oral—that injures another's reputation, fame or character is considered defamation. Individuals and companies both can be defamed. Unethical agents practice defamation by spreading rumors or falsehoods about the character of a competing agent or the financial condition of another insurance company. Both of these actions would be considered illegal in most states.

3. *Boycott, coercion or intimidation.* Agents and brokers are prohibited from acting in any manner that would lead the insurance prospect to believe that he or she must purchase from a particular agent, broker or company. For example, assume a real estate company also owns an insurance agency that offers homeowners coverage. A real estate broker may encourage his or her clients to purchase their insurance coverage from the agency, but an insurance agent cannot tell the prospective home buyers that their mortgage will not be approved *unless* they purchase insurance from the agency. Such an action could be considered coercion or intimidation.

4. *Twisting.* Virtually every jurisdiction prohibits the act of twisting and harshly penalizes any offender. Twisting is the unethical act of persuading a policyowner to drop a policy solely for the purpose of selling another policy, without regard to possible disadvantages to the policyowner. By definition, twisting involves some kind of misrepresentation by the agent to convince the policyowner to switch insurance companies and/or policies. Although twisting applies largely to life insurance policies, most states have regulations in place that require agents and brokers to provide policyowners with enough information to make an informed decision concerning the replacement of any existing policy.

5. *Replacement.* The unscrupulous act of twisting should not be confused with policy replacement. Again, most replacement regulations apply to life insurance but they may also apply to other policies. State laws recognize that sometimes a replacement may be in the policyowner's best interest, and they do not prevent an agent from replacing one insurance policy with another, provided the transaction is handled precisely in accordance with required procedures. These procedures include:

    - Full and fair disclosure of all facts regarding both the new coverage and the existing insurance. Policyowners who consider replacing policies should be fully aware of how the features of their existing policies are different from the replacement policies. They should also be made aware of any monetary penalties for cancellation or replacement of coverage.

- Proper completion of the appropriate forms by the agent. These forms must be signed by the insured, acknowledging that he or she is aware that coverage is being replaced by the new coverage being purchased. Typically this procedure includes returning the existing policy (or a signed *Lost Policy Release*) to the current insurer along with proof that a new insurance policy (in the form of a binder or a copy of the declarations page) is in force.

6. *Rebating.* As discussed in detail in Chapter 4, the subject of rebating commissions is an ongoing ethical debate. As you will recall, rebating occurs if the buyer of an insurance policy receives any part of the agent's commission or anything of significant value as an inducement to purchase the policy. In some states, a company or person convicted of a rebating violation is guilty of a misdemeanor. However, other states, such as California and Florida, permit agents or brokers to offer rebates under certain conditions.

Unfair Claims Settlement Practices

Few things will sour policyowners' opinions of their agent or agent's company more than the belief that they have been treated unfairly in a claim settlement. In fact, most consumer complaints involve claims—a company's refusal to pay a claim or its dispute about the amount payable to the claimant. State insurance codes offer some protection to insurance consumers in this important area and such complaints are often resolved in favor of the consumer. However, frequent consumer complaints have damaged the reputation of the insurance industry at large.

Most state insurance codes clearly identify certain claim settlement practices that are illegal. Commonly included in this group of illegal (and unfair) practices are the following:

- knowingly misrepresenting policy provisions to claimants or insureds at the time of claims;

- failing to acknowledge promptly pertinent communications concerning claims;

- failing to adopt and implement reasonable standards for settling claims;

- attempting to settle claims late and/or unfairly when the insurer's liability has become reasonably clear;

- failing to affirm or deny coverage of claims within a reasonable time after receiving proof of loss statements;

- attempting to settle a claim for less than could be reasonably expected, according to written or printed advertising material;

- failing to offer a reasonable and accurate explanation for denying a claim;

- compelling policyholders to go to court to recover amounts due them by offering them substantially less than the amounts that could be recovered by litigation;

- refusing to pay claims while conducting a reasonable investigation based on all available information;

- engaging in activities that result in a disproportionate number of complaints against the insurer received by the Department of Insurance;

- failing to provide necessary claim forms promptly, with explanations as to how to use them effectively; and

- engaging in any other acts that are equivalent in substance to any of the above listed acts.

Companies must affirm or deny liability on claims within a reasonable time and offer payment of approved claims within 30 days after affirming liability. Insurers are not to indicate that a payment draft represents a "final payment" or a "release" if additional benefit payments for the claim are probable under the policy, unless the policy limit has been paid or there is a bona fide dispute over the coverage or amount payable.

Also, a company may not require an insured to submit to a polygraph or similar type of examination as a condition to paying a claim. If a claim remains unresolved for 30 working days from the date reported, the company must provide the insured or, when applicable, the insured's beneficiary, with a reasonable written explanation for the delay.

Unfair Discrimination

It is illegal to permit *unfair discrimination* in the policy rates charged to individuals of the same risk classification. The key word here is "unfair." To a certain degree, discrimination exists in the underwriting of any insurance policy; two individuals of the same age, race and gender may represent very different risks to an insurer and will be charged different rates. For example, the rates for a 25-year-old man driving a 1984 Ford Escort will be quite different from one driving a 1995 Ford Mustang convertible, especially if the latter has two speeding tickets.

Unfair discrimination exists when two people of equal risk are charged different rates because of a difference in race, religion, national origin or where they live (*redlining*). Assume that two 25-year-old male neighbors, one white and one African American, both drive 1984 Ford Escorts four miles to work. If a company charges the African American driver more than the white driver, this is clearly a case of unfair discrimination and is illegal. It should be noted, however, that property and casualty insurers may charge different rates based on *territory* or *protection class*. These differentiations are based on company loss statistics and are not considered unfairly discriminatory.

ILL. 5.1 ■

Preventing Errors and Omissions Claims

Errors and omissions (E&O) insurance provides protection against loss incurred by a client because of some negligent act, error or omission by an insurance agent or broker, travel agent, real estate agent, attorney, consultant or other individual who gives advice to clients. An old adage is that insurance agents or brokers can prevent or reduce E&O claims by learning three new words: *document, document, document.* Regardless of the insurance transaction, the insurance professional should always make notes and keep up-to-date records about conversations with prospects and clients.

Experts suggest that producers can help to prevent or reduce E&O claims by following ten simple recommendations.

1. *Keep accurate records of all conversations, requests and details (such as who does what next) when dealing with prospects or clients.* Think defensively; take no shortcuts. If you are working in an agency, remember that an error on your part could negatively affect you, your employer and the insurance company you both represent.

2. *Develop and use standard forms and policies.* If possible, develop and use a procedures manual that documents each step in an agency process to reduce the possibility of human error.

3. *Take part in ongoing training.* Read trade publications, take continuing education classes and attend regular staff meetings to stay current on insurance topics.

4. *Put everything in writing, especially telephone conversations with insureds that require some action on your part.* Confirm the conversation by sending the insured a note and keeping a copy in the file. This may prevent misunderstandings should a claim arise in the future.

5. *Stay within your own area of expertise.* No one can expect to be an expert in every area. If your client asks you to quote on a coverage about which you know nothing, don't be afraid to say, "That's really not a subject with which I'm familiar, but two people in our agency specialize in that area. I'll put you in touch with them today."

6. *Listen to the client.* Remember that clients may be unfamiliar with insurance terminology and coverages. Pay attention to what the client is *really* saying. Summarize what you've heard and ask the client to confirm that you're correct.

7. *Avoid generalizations when discussing coverages.* No insurance policy or group of policies will protect a client against every peril or loss. Therefore, be careful about using sentences like: "This policy will take care of all your insurance needs." or "Our agency has a policy to meet any loss you might experience."

8. *Don't assume anything.* If you are an agency owner, insist that your employees become licensed and display their insurance licenses. If your agency uses sub-producers, don't assume that they carry their own E&O coverage; insist on proof of coverage.

9. *Use due diligence.* Investigate each insurance carrier you represent and be certain that it is financially stable and reliable. Understand its underwriting philosophy, claims procedures and reputation so that you can adequately explain them to your clients.

10. *Stay current.* Attend professional seminars, complete continuing education courses and read trade journals and other publications to be aware of the current regulatory trends that can affect your clients' policies.

This overview of state regulation of unethical conduct by insurance agents is but a sampling of the unfair practices defined by state insurance laws and the NAIC. Fortunately, unethical and dishonest agents are few and far between. But even honest agents must be careful not to succumb to temptation to maneuver the truth to land a big sale. Wrong decisions and inappropriate actions made under the pressure of the sales process can give rise to personal dissatisfaction and loss of integrity. Knowledge and calculated awareness can help the honest and ethical agent avoid many of the traps just outlined.

■ LICENSE SUSPENSION/TERMINATION

An unethical act can have severe repercussions because what most states consider unethical, they have also made illegal. In most states, an agent's license can be suspended or terminated for any of the following unethical actions:

1. making a materially untrue statement in the application for an agent's license;

2. violating or failing to comply with insurance laws in other states;

3. using fraud to obtain a license;

4. misappropriating funds;

5. misrepresenting the terms of a contract;

6. being convicted of a felony;

7. being convicted of an unfair trade practice;

8. having a license suspended in another state; or

9. engaging in fraudulent, coercive or dishonest practices, or being incompetent, untrustworthy or financially irresponsible.

In most states, an agent or broker whose license has been revoked may not apply for a new license for at least one year. Further, in many states, the insurance director or commissioner may stipulate that, as a condition of relicensing, the agent maintain a bond protecting the citizens of the state for at least five years.

■ PERSONAL VALUES AND ETHICS

An insurance producer's ethical responsibilities to the state in which he or she is licensed are set forth in statutes and regulations. In a way, each state creates a code of ethics by defining and codifying what is *not* legal and, by extension, *not* ethical. However, it would be wise not to confuse laws with ethics.

While laws set the minimum standard by which producers are expected to behave, a person's personal values or ethics provide a guidance system to help him or her choose the *right* answer or alternative to ethical dilemmas when several choices are available. In other words, laws tell us want we *must* do;

personal values and ethics, as defined by *what* we do, tell others what we believe in and who we are.

Personal Standards

Some people feel that ethics cannot be taught; you are either an ethical person or you're not. To some extent, this is true. However, all people have certain core beliefs and values, taught by their elders and established early in their lives, that dictate how they respond to certain situations or dilemmas. These values define who we are and what we believe in. The importance of maintaining a group's traditional beliefs are so important that some groups of people formulate their own written codes of ethics. For example, as shown in Ill. 5.2, some Native American tribes strengthen their values and beliefs by passing on the old ways and a shared community pride through both oral teachings and written codes of ethics. In this way, the next generation is taught to value and respect the importance of traditional beliefs, religious values, culture and language.

During our childhood, our values mirror those closest to us—family, friends and teachers—but they may change and shift as we grow older. In fact, people often adopt certain behaviors or beliefs that are in conflict with their own personal values in order to belong to a particular group. For example, assume a membership at a private tennis club, which specifically excludes people of certain races or religions, is a prerequisite for acceptance in your peer group and for a promotion at work. Your *personal* value system may condemn racism or elitism in any form, but your *professional* value system or "work ethic" may include doing whatever is necessary to advance in your career—working long hours, taking work home with you, joining the "right" clubs or organizations, etc. When personal and professional value systems conflict, one can experience a great deal of inner conflict.

People who set high personal and professional goals of honesty, integrity, loyalty, fairness, compassion, dependability, obedience to the law and truthfulness tend to experience more inner conflict than those who choose a lower path. Ethical people question the wisdom of taking questionable shortcuts, of beating the competition, of "winning" at all costs. They must find a way to achieve success at work without compromising their personal and professional values. One way to do this is to adhere to a strict code of professional ethics.

Professional Codes of Ethics

Laws and law enforcement develop from those values and principles that a society has internalized. Compliance with society's values was originally assured through application of peer pressure and the moral persuasion of the group as a whole or by the strength of its leaders. Creation of written laws and formal punishments for violating those laws came much later. However, given the fairly limited economic resources that a society can allocate to enforcement of every law, it is clear that any society must look to its members to formulate some sort of self-regulation in the form of codes of conduct or ethics.

Historically certain codes of ethics developed as a covenant among peers; however, modern codes of ethics have been based as well upon essential considerations of the public interest—especially with regard to trade and commercial relationships. Codes of ethics identify and encourage desirable activities by formally establishing a high standard against which each individual may measure

ILL. 5.2

> **Traditional Native Peoples Code of Ethics**
>
> 1. Give thanks to the Creator each morning upon rising and each evening before sleeping. Seek the courage and strength to be a better person.
> 2. Showing respect is a basic law of life.
> 3. Respect the wisdom of people in Council. Once you give an idea, it no longer belongs to you; it belongs to everyone.
> 4. Be truthful at all times.
> 5. Always treat your guest with honor and consideration. Give your best food and comforts to your guest.
> 6. The hurt of one is the hurt of all. The honor of one is the honor of all.
> 7. Receive strangers and outsiders kindly.
> 8. All races are children of the Creator and must be respected.
> 9. To serve others—to be of some use to family, community or nation—is one of the main purposes for which people are created. True happiness comes to those who dedicate their lives to the service of others.
> 10. Observe moderation and balance in all things.
> 11. Know those things that lead to your well-being and those things that lead to your destruction.
> 12. Listen and follow the guidance given to your heart. Expert guidance comes in many forms: In prayer, in dreams, in solitude and in the words and actions of elders and friends.

Source: *Win Awenen Nisitotung*, June 1994, Vol. 15, No. 6, p. 9.

his or her performance. Likewise, both the existence of these codes and the knowledge of these high standards discourage undesirable and unlawful activities by identifying conduct that is unacceptable to a particular group. In essence, codes of ethics can do a great deal to support and foster general social values through their ability to stimulate the education and self-regulation of industry members.

As stated in Chapter 1, most professions have written codes of ethics that pledge the members of the profession to certain standards of conduct. For example, in addition to having a broad understanding of accounting and tax laws, Certified Public Accountants (CPAs) must pass a series of rigorous examinations and are expected to adhere to a strict code of ethics. Because of the confidential and complex nature of their work, CPAs are held to a high level of professional conduct. Many other professional codes of conduct, such as the IIAA and CPCU codes, which are reprinted at the end of this text, are patterned after the CPA code of ethics.

CORPORATE ETHICS

The history of business in America might lead one to believe that the term "business ethics" is an oxymoron. Corporations have frequently been found guilty of self-interest, conflicts of interest, corruption, scandals, kickbacks, sexual harassment and a number of other illegal and immoral acts. Not surprisingly, the motive for high profit has often resulted in low ethical standards for some corporations. However, it is possible to apply personal values and ethics to the business arena without sacrificing the "bottom line."

Corporate ethics is simply the application of personal ethics to the corporate community, as well as a way to determine responsibility in business dealings. Business professionals are no different than other professionals in that they should abide by the strict principle spelled out clearly, 2,500 years ago, in the Hippocratic oath of the Greek physician: *primum non nocere* "First, do no harm." This basic rule of professional ethics should be closely followed by corporations and their employees, especially those "affected with the public interest," such as insurance professionals.

The Mission Statement

A corporation's goals and aspirations are spelled out in its corporate *mission statement*, a written declaration that provides a reference point for the intangible we call *corporate culture*. Most mission statements include some primary ethical standards and objectives for the business in which the company is engaged. A corporation's ethical standards might include some responsibility to its employees, clients, shareholders, suppliers and, in some cases, the general public. In general, the mission statement describes the company's commitment to these groups, rather than prescribing ethical conduct for particular situations.

For example, a company's mission statement might include the following as one of its primary ethical purposes: "We believe that our responsibility is to the local community, and we continue to strive toward serving the community in the best way possible." That statement would not, however, provide an answer to the ethical dilemma of choosing between building a new plant in the inner city where space is limited and expensive or in a rural area that offers space, a skilled labor force and tax incentives. The ethical dilemma for the company is whether to follow its stated "mission" and commit its resources to minority development in the local community or to "go for the bottom line" and build outside the community. The decision the corporation makes will show its true character, whether its stated concern for social welfare takes precedence over its profit motive.

Policies and Practices

The guiding principle behind every decision made by management is the corporation's policies and practices, whether written or unwritten. These policies and practices give the organization its particular structure and define its corporate culture. They define how things are done in the company and, as such, may be evaluated from an ethical perspective. Are the policies fair and just? Do they espouse desirable values and beliefs worthy of an ethical corporation? Or are they so nebulous that an unethical situation could unintentionally be created? Strategic plans about markets, products, cost reductions and the use of existing facilities are examples where ethical evaluations come into play.

One measurement of a corporation's understanding and practice of ethics is its response during times of crisis. Consider the example that Johnson & Johnson set for other companies in its rapid response to the crisis that arose when in 1982 several people in the Chicago area died after ingesting Tylenol with which someone had tampered. Johnson & Johnson immediately pulled its entire supply of Tylenol from every shelf in America—an expensive and unusual move at the time—demonstrating its concern for the health of the American public. The public responded by continuing to purchase Tylenol after the company introduced a series of tamper-proof containers. In fact, Johnson & Johnson's market share actually improved after its positive response to this tampering incident.

Some executives argue that ethical considerations cannot come into play in many business decisions because, under certain circumstances, the best interests of the corporation are in conflict with the interests of the public. For example, although some people see drug screening as an invasion of employee privacy and, by extension, an ethical issue, a corporation might argue that the right to screen for drug abuse is essential to maintaining a safe work place. In this case, the company feels that the safety of the entire work force is more important than an individual's right to privacy.

Business Codes of Ethics

As mentioned earlier, one way many professional organizations have attempted to address ethics is by establishing codes of ethics. This is no less true in the business environment. Business codes of ethics should clearly define the purpose of the organization, what it hopes to accomplish and how it plans to achieve those goals. Many corporations and trade organizations, such as the AFL-CIO, have written codes that are designed to guide, advise and regulate behavior on the job. Such codes are frequently included in personnel policy manuals and often reference activities such as conflicts of interest, proper use of company assets and property, compliance with the law and maintenance of a high standard of ethical conduct.

In order for codes of ethics to be effective, however, involvement and support must come from the top management of the corporation in the form of time, money and resources. If corporations expect their employees to follow certain codes of conduct, then management must lead by example. They should extend empathy, respect, fairness, loyalty and equity to their employees as well as their clients. In a best case scenario, the corporation will find a balance between the needs of its employees (i.e., respect, loyalty, trust) and the needs of the company (i.e., profits).

An Agent's or Broker's Code of Ethics

Insurance agents and brokers, by virtue of their chosen careers, act as independent contractors or businesses and may not always have a written code of ethics to guide them unless they have committed themselves to pursuing a professional designation and a professional code of ethics. They would also do well to develop their own personal code of ethics. In many cases, the agent or broker is involved in work which, at least some of the time, has to be done without the continuous support of colleagues. He or she may be working both inside and outside the office and the actual place of work may be remote or public. It is important for individuals to have fixed objectives and to monitor those objectives based on their own personal beliefs. For example, every person should have a set of standards or beliefs about how he or she should behave in order to be a good person.

Let's look at an example of how a person's beliefs behavior can affect the way in which he or she handles a job situation.

Assume that Karen Jones is an agent for Hemisphere Agency. Karen was hired as an agent when Hemisphere learned that Karen's general attitude was "To be a good insurance agent I must never show any signs of weakness. To show weakness means I am not up to the job." A major part of Karen's job as an insurance agent is to obtain regular payments from a number of clients at their business premises. Usually the payments are ready for her but occasionally she has to get tough and demand payment. She always returns to the agency with cash or a check from the client.

The elements of Karen's job are quite simple: she must visit her clients regularly, keep accurate records, be completely trustworthy with the premiums she collects and be confident and competent in her role as a premium collector. Now, assume that Karen has not developed a strong set of personal standards or beliefs that include honesty, integrity, decency and respect. Her largest client pays Karen with a certified check for $50,000 for his commercial policies. Karen, who has incurred personal bills amounting to over $35,000, opts for instant gratification and in her own self-interest, cashes the check and pays her bills. She's certain that she'll be able to reimburse the agency in the near future.

However, if Karen had developed high personal standards, she would find it difficult (or impossible) to place her own interests above the client or the agency. And, if Karen does inadvertently do something to harm her agency or client, she will feel that she has violated her own personal code of conduct.

As noted in this chapter, however formal or informal the process is to establish the rules for ethical conduct, the rules still do not go beyond common sense and natural integrity. These attributes, plus knowledge and calculated awareness, can help the ethical agent steer clear of many temptations. Our next chapter discusses some practical methods to help you avoid such pitfalls.

■■■■■ Ethical Issue Number Five

"PACKAGE 1 OR PACKAGE 2"

Mike and Anita Sanchez own ten townhomes as rental units in the Estes Park Community, located in a lower income, racially mixed section of town. Over the years, the Sanchezes have become well-known for renting to minority and disabled singles and to couples who are down on their luck. For the past six years, Andy Rice has been their insurance agent and trusted friend. But Andy has decided to retire within a few weeks so the Sanchezes want to shop their insurance and to look around for a new agent who can offer them the same (or better) coverage, service and premium.

After meeting with a number of other agents, the Sanchezes have decided to allow both Marie Howe, who has worked with Andy for years and is taking over his accounts, and Charlie Michaels, an agent with the National Agency, to provide quotes on their rental properties. Having trust in Andy's knowledge and professionalism, the Sanchezes have asked Andy to provide a review of the two quotes and make his recommendations. They have agreed to accept the coverage that Andy believes is best for them.

Charlie Michaels has two programs available for rental property owners. Both programs are written through the New World Insurance Company, and although they are identical in underwriting and contract provisions, they have different commission rates: 10 percent for the Property Owners Package (POP) and 15 percent for the Landlord/Rental Package (LRP). Although many agencies choose to sell only one of the programs, National Agency sells both, allowing the agent to select which one to present to the prospect. Charlie quoted the LRP program, which provides similar coverages to Marie's proposed renewal with Old World Insurance, but at a slightly less expensive premium.

Although Andy wants Marie to keep the Sanchez account, he also knows that the best deal for the client should be considered. Both companies offer virtually the same coverages, but New World's premium is less. Yet Andy is not comfortable with Charlie's proposal. He knows, for example, that Charlie has written contracts in the Property Owners Package (POP) program for other insureds, but only those in middle-class suburbs. He also knows that, because the underwriting requirements are the same in both programs, Charlie could have presented to the Sanchezes, a quote in the lower commissioned POP program—saving them about 5 percent on their annual premium.

Andy wants to finish his evaluation early in order to review it carefully and be ready for his afternoon meeting with Mike and Anita Sanchez. However, he isn't sure how to deal with this situation. He doesn't want to appear to be bad-mouthing Charlie just so Marie can keep the renewal. He sits looking out of his window, wondering how to present his recommendation.

Your Comments Please

1. What are the legal issues involved in this case?

2. What are the ethical issues involved in this case?

3. What would you do if you where Andy?

4. How would you balance "making money" with "providing service"?

6 Practical Answers to Ethical Questions

Thus far, our study has concentrated on the ethical and legal issues an agent may face in his or her daily activity. We have also covered some of the penalties for those who fail to meet these challenges. However, those who aspire to a higher degree of professionalism need to know more than what *has* to be done. They must also understand the elements of ethical decision making that will give them an added perspective. This chapter focuses on practical methods an insurance producer can use to meet his or her ethical and legal responsibilities to the insurance industry, insurers, clients and public. These approaches add the dimension of knowledge and awareness for the agent who wants to go "the extra mile" to achieve ethical and professional excellence.

■ ETHICAL DECISION MAKING

Even though it may not always seem to be so, there is an obvious connection between business and ethics. A businessperson whose employees steal from him or her could no more survive than one who through lying and fraud sold only products that did not work. In the short run, lying, fraud, deception and theft may lead to greater profits than honesty and truthfulness. However, actions that are contrary to accepted ethical standards are bad for business in the long run because they run counter to the common good. Eventually, either legal measures or public pressures will impose penalties on wrongdoers that make the immoral or unethical practices unprofitable. If the penalties for acting illegally or unethically are severe enough, conforming to high ethical standards will eventually be in the best interest of business, employees, clients and society in general. But who decides what is ethical?

Discussions of ethical decision making often begin by asking three questions. First, whose ethics are to be imposed on the insurance industry? Second, can economic systems be morally evaluated, and how does this evaluation apply to different economic systems and different cultures with different norms? Third, which specific practices within a given system are in the public's good?

All three questions assume that morality differs from person to person, that each person's principles are equally valid and that somehow one must choose the "right" set of ethics. The questions also presume that somehow "individuals" are different from "businesses" and, therefore, different standards of conduct apply where businesses are concerned. This argument is often used because corporations, as business entities rather than individuals, have no "conscience." The general public also seems to believe that because corporations are usually in business to make money, they have no compunction about lying, cheating or stealing to enhance the bottom line. In fact, many people quote that old saying "nice guys finish last" and argue that dealing honestly with clients can actually doom a business.

From our previous discussion, it should be clear that nearly every society agrees that good should be done and that evil should be avoided in order for the society to survive. Most societies value respect for the lives of their members, for the truth and for cooperation between the group's members. Although many nations will easily go to war with another nation and kill hundreds of other people, those same nations find it immoral for an ordinary member of their society to kill another member. Such an act is often punishable by death. In other words, regardless of where a society exists, societies tend to share the belief that there are ways to measure and reward "good" and to punish "evil."

As stated previously, the insurance industry is highly regulated by the government. However, the state insurance codes lack uniformity and are often complex or difficult to understand. Therefore, the industry voluntarily complies with certain standards of self-regulation set by a number of insurer and trade associations. For example, the Insurance Services Office files policy forms and rates for approval by the state insurance departments for many fire, automobile, liability and other types of insurance carriers. This saves time and reduces the insurers' costs. Other organizations, such as the Insurance Institute for Highway Safety and the National Association of Insurance Brokers, regulate marketing activities. Still other organizations, such as the American College, the American Institute for Chartered Property Casualty Underwriters and the Independent Insurance Agents of America, offer insurance education and set standards for professional courses and designations. Such industry organizations help agents and brokers formulate answers to a number of ethical dilemmas, even though each situation has many unique aspects and considerations to be weighed.

Important Ethical Questions

Ethical decision making is a process of asking yourself several important questions about the situation in which you are involved. As with any difficult decision, these questions entail serious reflection and require the agent or broker to think broadly about the implications of his or her actions. In each situation, the producer should consider the following four questions:

1. To whom do I have obligations and what are these obligations?

2. Who has rights that must be protected?

3. What moral rules apply to this situation and should be upheld?

4. Would I be proud of my decision and publicly advocate this action?

Take some time to answer these questions specifically and thoughtfully as you consider the following two ethical issues.

Ethical Issue #1: You worked very hard on an insurance proposal for commercial insurance coverage for a newly constructed apartment building. The prospect felt she couldn't afford the original policy you recommended, and you had to work through five other proposals before she agreed to purchase the commercial package policy you presented yesterday. You explained the renewal provisions of the policy, but deep down you suspect she didn't really understand the coverages. Should you call her back and review the policy provisions, or just send the application in to the company and forget it?

Ethical Issue #2: You've known Dan since high school, and he became one of your first homeowners insurance policyowners. Now, he wants to switch his auto coverage to your agency at renewal. Both Dan and his wife drive expensive sports cars that will generate some substantial premium for your agency. If you can write this business, you'll qualify for an additional bonus this quarter.

You've completed the paperwork for the company; Dan has signed the application and given you a deposit premium. Coverage will go into effect in three days when Dan's current policy expires. As you are putting the application and check in a company envelope, Dan calls and tells you that he has just had an auto accident downtown and wants to know if that will cause any problem with the coverage he applied for with you.

You know that the police reports and claims paperwork will take at least a week before becoming public knowledge. If Dan goes to court and is determined to be at fault, it will be at least 30 days before the accident will appear on his Motor Vehicle Report (MVR). If you mail the application today and the casualty underwriter immediately requests an MVR, it will probably be clean and the policy will be issued.

What do you do? Send in the application today? Or call Dan back and explain that your quote assumed that he had had no tickets or accidents within the past three years?

Both of these issues involve situations in which ethical decision making will determine the outcome. As an agent, you could easily walk away and let events take their course. However, you also know that whatever you do, your professional future is involved. Your action will depend upon your professionalism and personal ethics, each of which is based on the following traits: *character, competence, attitude* and *sense of purpose*.

Let's take a closer look at these traits.

Character

In an essay on spiritual laws, Ralph Waldo Emerson said: "Human character evermore publishes itself. The most fugitive deed and word, the mere air of doing a thing, the intimated purpose, expresses character. If you act you show character: if you sit still, if you sleep, you show it." What Emerson is saying is that people judge us by what they see and hear us do. Our every action (or inaction) indicates to others just who we are. Ultimately insurance professionals are judged by what they stand for—their values, priorities, ethics—their *character*.

What is a prime characteristic of character? *Honesty* leads the list, but the word "character" also encompasses several other virtues—integrity, dependability, discipline, truthfulness. Each time you encounter a conflict or dilemma, ask yourself, "How can I be fair and honest in my dealings with others in this situation? Whose interests are being served here—my client's, my company's or my own? Am I being dishonest?"

In today's fast-paced business environment it may seem old-fashioned to cultivate one's character; however, no one gets anywhere in the insurance business without personal integrity. Certainly there are amoral and self-serving people who are financially successful. But if you look back at your own career and that of other agents, you'll discover that those who lacked integrity did not last very long in the business. Producers who are involved in illegal schemes or who accept kickbacks as part of writing business do so because they opt for temporary success; it provides them with instant gratification. Their focus on achieving short-term goals at the expense of their personal ethics fails to provide long successful insurance careers.

Knowledge, skill and circumstances do not control long-term success as much as who the person is, what he or she stands for and what guides the person. We all know at least one person who is the essence of honesty and integrity. When he or she says something it is true, we believe it. We trust that person because of their moral fiber. Because confidential information from the insured is usually required in order to provide the needed insurance protection, the agent's or broker's relationship with the insured is similar to the confidential relationship between an individual and his or her physician, lawyer or accountant. The prospect or client must believe that the agent or broker can be trusted with that confidential information.

Just like some athletes who don't have a great deal of natural ability but who ultimately succeed through hard work and discipline, insurance professionals can achieve success through discipline, commitment to excellence and perseverance. There can be no sense of purpose, no progress, no real balance unless the foundation of daily activity is personal integrity.

Competence

Before you tackle each new risk, do you feel that you can competently handle it? Do the insurance companies you represent have the coverages and personnel to handle the special needs of your client base? Do you have the skills, knowledge and training to do what has to be done to provide your prospect or client with the best coverage at the most competitive price?

Competence comes from training and experience. Agents and brokers have a two-fold job: (1) learning about the prospect's insurance needs and (2) helping the insurance buyer to understand and appreciate the value of the service they are being given. A competent agent or broker provides a wide variety of services that are essential to providing the proper insurance coverage. Before the sale, these services include discovering and analyzing significant risks, providing loss control or inspection services, finding appropriate insurance markets, confirming the accuracy of the classification and the rates charged and comparing alternative coverages offered by other insurers. After the sale, these services include continued loss control services, assistance in settling claims promptly, reviewing changing insurance needs and making recommendations to meet those needs.

Few agents know all the answers to every question that a client may raise—especially if the risk is an unusual one for a small agency, such as a U.S. manufacturer who has several factories in Mexico. There is no embarrassment in lacking some knowledge or skill you need to competently handle a particular risk. If you lack the experience you need to initially underwrite or service the risk, you can find help from more experienced colleagues, a company underwriter, a loss control expert or a risk manager. You may also have to recommend additional legal, accounting or consulting services to your client when they are needed. The ethical violation occurs when you *pretend* that you have skill and knowledge when, in fact, you do not, or if you ignore the need to complete the education and training necessary to identify, analyze and treat a risk properly.

In addition to completing continuing education requirements to maintain their licenses, many insurance producers work toward professional designations, such as *Certified Insurance Counselor (CIC)* or *Chartered Property Casualty Underwriter (CPCU)*. As you increase your competency and gain experience, you'll find that you'll be able to answer more and more questions, and still know when to ask the experts.

Attitude

What is your attitude toward the insurance business? How do you feel about your clients? Your agency? Your company? Your competition? All of these feelings create your general attitude toward others. If you feel a sense of service toward your clients, company and business, you're likely putting someone else's interests ahead of your own. An ethical code of conduct calls for you to set aside your own interests and concentrate on doing what has to be done to help your client or prospect. You'll be satisfied that you've done the right thing and that kind of satisfaction, above all, is the mark of a true professional.

Sense of Purpose

The last section of this text includes codes of ethics of various insurance industry associations. Each of these codes denotes the sense of purpose for that particular organization and prescribes what should be done to raise the level of professionalism for all.

There is no tried-and-true checklist to help you determine your own sense of purpose. That can only come from you and your personal values. However, for those seeking personal and professional guideposts worth pursuing, here's a list of questions they can ask themselves:

1. Have I withheld information from a client or insurer?

2. Have I obtained information from someone and used that information for my own personal benefit?

3. Have I made disparaging remarks about another agent, insurer or professional?

4. Have I competed fairly or unfairly?

5. Have I misrepresented the benefits, the premium or the limitations of a policy I recommended?

PRACTICAL WAYS TO AVOID TROUBLE

Even an ethical insurance agent can find trouble in today's world. The complexities of some insurance needs can be addressed by several insurance plans and even a sound recommendation made by an agent with confidence could fail to meet the client's expectations. Unfortunately, in our litigious society, disenchanted policyowners and injured parties may seek a remedy that includes retaining an attorney.

What can an ethical agent do to protect himself or herself? The answers are many:

- rely on his or her practice of personal ethics;

- purchase personal errors and omissions insurance to provide financial protection against claims;

- perform due care when recommending policies and placing business; and

- be committed to a program of continuing education.

Personal Ethics

Assume that the Jones family complains to the state insurance commissioner and to the insurer that Agent John Murphy committed professional malpractice because he did not perform his duties to the extent the Joneses believed he should have. The Joneses are certain that when Mr. Murphy sold them their homeowners coverage, he called it an "all risk" policy and never explained that certain perils, such as earthquake, are excluded under the form. When the family's house was damaged by an earthquake, the insurer denied the claim. The Joneses feel that Murphy was negligent in selling them a policy that excludes earthquake and, therefore, should be held personally responsible for the damage to their house.

What can John Murphy say in his own defense to prove that he handled the account in the proper way? What are some of the provable acts that he should cite to prove that he acted in a legal and ethical manner? Agent Murphy can begin by asking himself the following questions.

#1: How Well Did Agent Murphy Perform His Duty?

To answer this question, remember that what you as an agent are required to do for someone and, conversely, what you are required *not* to do is spelled out in your agency contract. Also pertinent is what was agreed to by you and the client. Finally, the rules of your state and the customs of the insurance industry apply.

ILL. 6.1 ■

Ethical Guideposts

The four building blocks of ethics—character, competence, attitude and sense of purpose—will help determine your actions or responses to any given situation. In addition, as a practical tool, Professor Robbin Derry of the American College has developed a series of practical ethics questions that the professional agent can use as a guide before he or she decides how to handle an ethical dilemma. These questions are:

1. Can the action I am about to take stand the light of publicity?

Imagine that the action you are about to take is featured on national television. A press conference is scheduled for 10:00 A.M. tomorrow to scrutinize your action. Could you explain your motives, your role in the event, with pride? If you can't, reexamine what you're planning to do.

2. To whom do I owe an obligation in this case?

Remember, an insurance agent owes several obligations: to his or her insurance company as its agent; to the policyowner and the public as a fiduciary of the insured; and to the community that looks to the agent both as an insurance professional and a private citizen. However, this does not mean that the agent must be all things to all parties. There are times when the agent's duties are specifically those as agent of the insurer.

3. What is the obligation that I owe?

The agent has to sort out what obligations he or she has as the case progresses. What has the agent promised? To whom has he or she made that promise? Why was the promise made?

4. Who has rights that must be protected?

It is quite common for an agent to work with several members of the same family. Conflicts of interest may come up over tax elections, interpretations and the exercise of authority. In these instances, the agent's best way to handle things is to provide full disclosure. However, the rights of all involved must be protected—as well as the rights of the agent's insurer.

5. Is this action a breach of my ethical duty? To my company? To the policyowner?

An agent must adhere to the terms of his or her agency agreement, as well as to the overall duty of loyalty to the insurer. With regards to the client, the agent owes the duty of honesty, competency and loyalty to the client.

Whereas these questions are not guaranteed to solve the dilemma, they should provide guidelines. In addition, the agent must determine the issues that will demand ethical conduct. Identifying ethical issues and using guidelines such as these should help the agent practice sound ethics on a day-to-day basis.

If Murphy can show to everyone's satisfaction that he performed his duties in this situation according to the standards imposed upon him by all parties, his defense is solid. For example, assume that Agent Murphy quotes only the ISO HO-3 form because he believes it to be the best coverage for his clients. During every homeowners sales presentation Murphy points out that the term "all risk" is really a misnomer because the form contains some exclusions and limitations. In fact, Murphy gives every prospect a written explanation of the limitations and exclusions contained in the HO-3 form and specifically asks whether the prospect might need additional coverage, such as a jewelry floater. He also encourages clients and prospects to read their policies and to call his office with any questions.

#2: Did Agent Murphy Avoid His Duty?

An agent's requirement of duty to his or her client consists of three factors: his or her fiduciary relationship to the client; the agent's legal duty; and his or her reasonable care in conducting insurance business.

If Murphy can show that no breach of his duty in any of these areas took place and can prove he carried out his duty with reasonable care, his defense, again, is solid. For example, assume that the client wants the most comprehensive coverage available at the lowest premium. In order to do this, Murphy provides quotes from all his standard carriers, explains the differences among the companies and suggests Ironclad Insurance. The clients accept and sign the homeowners application, provide a picture of the dwelling and write a personal check for the first annual premium. According to the terms of his agency agreement, Murphy must forward these items to Ironclad within five working days of the effective date of coverage. Murphy follows these requirements for every new application and, therefore, fulfills his duty to his clients, the insurer and the law.

#3: Can Agent Murphy Show Reasonable Care?

An extension of the above, reasonable care is the level to which an agent carries out his or her duty. Ethical agents can document reasonable care if they can show that:

1. They determined the needs of the client.

2. They sold to those needs.

3. They presented a plan to meet those needs, as well as alternatives if the client expressed dissatisfaction with the original plan.

4. Their recommendations and the client's ultimate decision are in writing.

Errors and Omissions Insurance

As explained in Chapter 5, one measure of protection adopted by many agency managers and agents is *errors and omissions insurance* (E&O). Under this type of liability protection, the agent or agency is the insured and is covered for legal defense and settlement costs (up to a stipulated maximum) stemming from professional services he or she rendered or failed to render. The unlicensed employees of the agency or agent can also be covered as long as they do not carry an agent's or broker's contract and do not produce new business.

The professional services E&O insurance covers the sale of insurance and employee benefit plans, along with the advice and administrative activities associated with or for the agent's or agency's plans.

Excluded from coverage are any actions that:

- are committed through fraud or criminal intent;
- are covered under any other contract or agreement; or
- are caused by misuse of client funds.

Errors and omissions insurance is available on an individual or group basis. Premiums for the coverage are generally determined by whether the state in which coverage is to be provided is a high-risk or low-risk state.

Whether or not this coverage is needed is an individual decision for the agent or agency manager and is usually based on perceived exposure to lawsuits in the community. If it is likely that a claim can be brought against the agent or agency, errors and omissions insurance may be a prudent buy.

Due Care

With the solvency of many financial institutions an open question today, the insurance agent is often called on to inform a policyowner or prospective policyowner about the financial condition of the insurance company behind the policy the agent is recommending.

The description many would attach to this duty is *due diligence,* a term used in the securities industry. It refers to the legal requirement that a securities representative furnish full documentation on the financial health of a company whose stocks, bonds or other financial instruments are offered for purchase. In this case, full and complete documentation can be made because financial information is readily available through corporate reports, financial plans, research documents and other financial material required by federal and state laws.

In the insurance industry, it is the duty of the state insurance department to provide financial information since it is with the insurance department that an insurer files required financial reports. An agent's only legal obligation is

- to sell the policies of the insurance companies licensed in the state where applications are taken; and
- *not* to sell the policies of companies known by the agent to be insolvent.

So, in contrast to due diligence and the strict legal requirements it entails, the insurance industry generally advocates that an agent adopt a policy of *due care* in his or her dealings with clients and prospects. Under due care, providing complete and valid information to a client is regarded as an essential part of client service and the agent will make every effort to obtain this financial information when prospective clients or prospects request it.

Agents who wish to practice due care and provide current financial information about an insurer should start with the insurer itself. Additional information can be obtained from other independent sources, including the state insurance department.

Continuing Education

In the insurance business, increased knowledge equals greater competence. Many agents today work or plan to work in specialized markets. In these specialized markets there are many insurance policies available that can be redesigned to meet clients' needs. For example, agents active in the commercial insurance business have a variety of traditional policies available to cover domestic risks; however, many of these policies do not address rather recent business developments, such as international or global coverage, environmental impairment issues or the possibility of a corporate kidnapping. The agent must be aware of any new policies with new features that are introduced regularly in the property-casualty field to address these and other unusual risks.

Insurance agents have to understand the features of these policies, their benefits, limitations and exclusions. In addition, agents also have to know how these products compare to other policies their insurer offers as well as how they compare to products of other insurance companies. In personal lines insurance, the individual or entire family may be interested in knowing the specifics of the plan being recommended. In commercial insurance, the differences in policies and coverages are of special interest to the CEO, risk manager and/or corporate attorney, who are the usual decision makers on such programs.

The only way an insurance agent can maintain his or her expertise in a chosen market is through continued training in products and legislative changes affecting the policies the agent represents. General business courses, for example, would not be applicable in most states. The agent must keep current with new product offerings and new policy features that could benefit clients.

Whether or not continuing education is mandated to keep one's license in effect, the prudent agent will pursue expertise in specialized policies and markets. Continuing education enhances a person's professionalism and credibility.

■ GUIDELINES FOR ETHICAL DECISION MAKING

Agents often feel that many of the ethical challenges confronting them stem from two sources: competition and the stress of performance quotas. Agents note that the intense competition within the insurance industry as a whole forces management to look at the bottom line, creating a conflict with business ethics, as does the competition agents face individually. Furthermore, agents think that the practice of measuring performance on the basis of end results and production quotas poses a challenge to ethics since the result is considered more important than the means.

Solutions to the ethical conflicts that can be traced to the business environment begin with agency or insurance home office guidance and training in business ethics. For example, a home office senior officer's main function might be to develop an insurance company code of ethics. This officer would also supervise and monitor agents' activity, investigating all field reports of unethical activity. This senior officer would also provide a clear communication channel of appropriate ethical behavior from company management to the agents representing the insurer.

Above all, ethical agents stress the need for an agency environment that does not encourage an agent to compromise his or her ethical standards just to achieve a goal. If the insurers they represent also emphasize ethics in business situations, this would help strengthen agents' resolve in dealing with the ethical issues that confront them. Ethics training courses and a regular opportunity for group discussion in the agency would be welcome.

Personal and Professional Attributes

Throughout this text we've emphasized that the most important factor for an individual agent in dealing with ethical challenges is his or her own personal moral values and standards. The person looking back at you in the mirror is the best judge of what should be done in a given ethical situation. Family and friends can provide support and insight to help resolve ethical conflicts, as can the agency manager or principal, but it is still the individual agent, using his or her standards of proper ethical behavior, who must respond to the ethical challenge.

From the beginning of this course, we have discussed the need for an insurance agent's personal code of ethical standards. This is important not only for the insurance industry, but also for the company or companies the agent represents in the community. On the philosophical level, the agent needs a code to maintain his or her own dignity and self-esteem. A personal code of ethics will help create a better, more prosperous insurance agent along with a better, more prosperous insurance company and a better, more prosperous insurance industry.

No one can hope for a better future than that.

■■■■■ Ethical Issue Number Six

"HOUSEWARMING"

Susan Harrison was very excited. As a newly licensed agent at the B&G Agency, she was given her own book of current business for renewals. She was determined to visit each client, introduce herself and make sure that the vast majority renewed with her.

Elliot and Sara Leat had been living in an apartment for many years, and B&G provided renters coverage. The day Susan stopped by the apartment to talk to them about updating and renewing their coverage, they had just arranged to close on the house of their dreams.

"Susan," Elliot said, "we were going to call the agency tomorrow. We need to have an insurance policy on the new house for the closing. Can you do that?"

"Sure can," Susan said while ferreting through her briefcase in search of an application. With an application and her rate book in hand, Susan gave the Leats a quote for an HO-3 policy. Susan smiled and said, "The HO-3 form is a standard contract. It will cover the house and everything in it on an all-risk basis, and it also includes $100,000 in personal liability coverage."

Sara was anxious to finish the deal and move into her new home. "You mean it covers everything, Susan? That's great, but do we really need $100,000 in liability insurance? Isn't that too much?"

"No," explained Susan, "that is the minimum we can write. We can write up to $1 million if you want, but I don't think you need it. Now, you'll need to show a paid-up policy at the closing, so I'll need a check for $458.00."

Elliot was looking at the paperwork from the realtor and his checkbook. "No can do," Elliot said. "We close next week and I don't get paid until the end of the month. I'll end up almost $300 short for the closing." He looked at this wife for help.

Susan was determined to keep the business. "I'll tell you what," she said. "I'll front the money for the premium on the homeowners policy with the understanding that I also write your automobile insurance. I will have your new homeowners policy ready for you in two days. Make a check payable to me for $100 and pay me the balance on the first of next month. Does that help?"

Elliot and Sara agreed and signed the homeowners application. The check, made out to "Susan Harrison" was deposited in Susan's personal checking account, and Susan then wrote a check for the annual premium to the insurance company, net the commission, five days later. The policy was delivered when promised and the closing went off without a hitch.

On the second of the following month, Susan visited the Leats at their new home and collected the remainder of the premium. She also brought them a crystal vase as a housewarming gift. She asked the Leats to give her the information she needed to write their auto insurance. Elliot was so pleased with the way Susan handled their account that he introduced her to the real estate agent for more leads.

Your Comments Please

1. There are at least four possible ethical and/or legal violations. Please list them.

   _____
   _____
   _____
   _____
   _____

2. One of these possible violations could be based on "perception." Please identify the situation and the possible conflict.

   _____
   _____
   _____
   _____
   _____

3. If you were Susan's supervisor, how would you deal with this situation?

   _____
   _____
   _____
   _____
   _____

Guidelines to Ethical Issues

The following pages contain the analyses of the ethical issues found at the end of the text chapters and illustrative Codes of Ethics of the Independent Insurance Agents of America and the American Institute for Chartered Property Casualty Underwriters.

Analysis

Ethical Issue Number One

One of the biggest problems agents face is balancing personal relationships with their responsibilities to the insurance companies they represent. In addition, there is a question of law, because many states have insurance fraud statutes on the books. Those states that do not carry such a statute revert back to the state's anticrime or fraud laws.

Martin is a licensed producer in Pennsylvania with an agency agreement with Penn/General. This agency agreement states, in very specific terms, that Martin and those who work for him in the Bethany Agency, are an extension of the company. They have the right to solicit, underwrite and bind coverage as well as collect premium and, in some cases, cancel insurance contracts. Though his ability to act on the company's behalf is limited to the Pennsylvania state line, the knowledge he acquires outside of his home state may be pertinent to the company's operation and should be reported.

Some individuals might suggest that because the incident occurred outside Pennsylvania, Martin has no duty to report the incident to Penn/General. Others might weigh the factors—the amount of the damages, the cost of the damage, the cost of losing a friendship. If this is the case, they might feel the situation changes if the claims payment were increased to $500, $1,000 or $2,500. However, neither the place where the accident occurred nor the amount of the payment should affect Martin's decision. He knows that there has been a misrepresentation of material fact and that fraud has been committed—whether in the amount of $450 or $2,500.

Martin should first explain to Randall that it is simply *not right* to keep something that doesn't belong to him or to profit from the misfortune of others and then suggest a possible solution of returning the $200 for the bumper. (The $250 settlement for the fender and wheel alignment was justified.) Or Martin, if he felt so inclined, could report the indiscretion to the local claims supervisor, identifying himself as an agent from another state. Or he could discuss the situation with a contact at Penn/General (the marketing manager, for example). Any of these solutions may satisfy the ethical obligation of all agents to act honestly, loyally and in good faith toward their insurers and to reveal to the insurer all material facts concerning the agency relationship.

■■■■■ *Analysis*

Ethical Issue Number Two

The initial problems are self-evident: Robert has overextended the agency, has not recognized the problem and is now working in a negative cash flow situation. In an attempt to rectify this "cash flow problem," both Robert and June are in possible violation of a number of laws and general principles for insurance agencies conducting the business of insurance.

The ethical problems here include:

1. the overextension of the cash flow;

2. the agency's fiduciary responsibility to the company(ies);

3. the commingling of funds;

4. the agency's fiduciary responsibility to the consumer; and

5. June's active knowledge and participation.

In most states, the law requires that an insurance agent who invoices clients must remit that premium (less commissions and return premium due clients) to the insurance company by the contractual due date (the first, fifteenth or last day of the month) or within 45 days of the date the premium was received. By asking June to place the premium into a certificate of deposit for two 30-day periods, Robert will not be able to meet either of these provisions.

The second problem is the commingling of the premiums collected with the general account fund of the agency. Once again, this is not an acceptable action and a possible violation of state law. Most states require that premiums be held in a separate account, with any interest received to be applied directly to the operations of the office. Although commingling may not seem like a major problem, most insurance departments see the practice as a sign of other possible financial problems with the agency.

The third problem is the fiduciary responsibility Robert and June have to the clients whose policies were canceled. Not only is the agent required to return funds to the former insured within a reasonable time (45 days), but he or she must refund to the insurer a portion of the commission originally paid to the agent when the policy was issued. By delaying these payments and/or not refunding the commission to United, Robert is committing a very serious ethical and legal violation. Because June is also a licensed agent with United, she is guilty of the same violations.

The insurance department will not permit cancellation for nonpayment of any of the insurance contracts placed through the Flatiron Agency, if the insured can show that he or she paid the agency for the insurance. Robert represents The

United; therefore, payment to Robert is, in fact, payment to The United. The department of insurance would not permit the insured to suffer (i.e., have the insurance canceled for nonpayment) and would prevent the insurance company from taking such action when the agent has been paid.

Good business practices are essential to the operation of an insurance agency, no matter how small or large. As the agency owner and principal, Robert should seek to ease the total burden by limiting the usage of the car telephones to business. He and his salespeople might consider using their own personal automobiles for business, and the vacations at the agency's expense should be eliminated. Robert may also consider returning to the local college and completing a few courses in general small business management and accounting.

Analysis

Ethical Issue Number Three

The Millers face questions of ethics, law and agency as they struggle with this situation. As licensed agents with Atlas, they are considered "the company," and knowledge they receive should be forwarded to the proper department at Atlas. In addition, by telling the Hannocks that they should not report the claim, Liz and Bill are creating a situation that directly contradicts the conditions section of the insurance contract. There is also the potential issue of a material misrepresentation on an insurance application and the possibility of fraud.

Though fraud is a possibility, it can only be determined by a court of appropriate jurisdiction. *Fraud* is defined as a purposeful misrepresentation of fact to induce action that would cause injury (physical, financial or legal) to a third party. In this case, though the misrepresentation would not cause immediate damage to the new homeowners insurer. But it does create a problem with adverse selection, which may eventually cause an overall increase in premiums for all insureds.

Many states have specific statutes and regulations concerning the cancellation of a homeowners insurance contract. These laws are designed to protect the insured by allowing a reasonable amount of time to replace the coverage, prevent cancellation or nonrenewal for unreasonable situations and, in some cases, provide a recourse to the proposed action. Check your state laws to determine the extent of these rules. Even if your state does not have a Fair Plan, there are xcess and surplus lines markets that will write the coverage.

The balance between friendship, client loyalty and obligation to the company is a difficult one at best. When the balance is upset by what you feel is a possible "unjust action," then you may want to consider removing yourself from the immediate decision. In some cases, the account could be transferred to another agent in the office or to a supervisor to handle the situation. In all situations, the agent must remember that his or her loyalty is to the insurer, not the insured. If there is a legal recourse, you should advise your client to initiate that action prior to your becoming their advocate. In this way, you do not jeopardize their legal rights under your state's insurance laws.

The Millers have raised some interesting issues that Andy Martinez might use in future classes as examples of ethical issues that agents face. He might also be able to give them an unbiased viewpoint. Andy should advise the Millers to remember that, despite their perception about the unfairness of the law, insurance rules and regulations were developed to enhance the fair treatment of *all* parties involved in similar situations. Violations of these rules could result in fines, the suspension or revocation of licenses and certificates of authority and, in some states, jail. With these as added factors, it would appear that the Millers have no choice but to advise the Hannocks to report the claims, to complete an application with another carrier as completely and honestly as possible and to seek coverage for their client for the best possible price available.

Of course, it is possible that the Atlas will not cancel the homeowners policy. In this case, it might be in the Hannocks' best interest to remain with their current homeowners agent. And, if the Millers wish to act in the best interest of their friends, they might even suggest that the Hannocks move their auto coverage to the agency that currently writes their homeowners coverage. Some companies offer a premium discount on both the homeowners and auto coverage when the company writes both policies.

What the Millers owe the Hannocks is complete honesty and openness about the situation, the possible ramifications of not reporting a claim (or misrepresenting their loss history on an application for insurance) and suggestions on how these problems can be resolved. To do less could create a true personal ethical dilemma.

Analysis

Ethical Issue Number Four

As with many agents, especially those who have unusual or specialized knowledge in one area, there is a pride in being able to handle any situation that comes along. Many seasoned agents, however, will tell you that the use of "experts" or authorities who can assist in the underwriting of new risks or risks in areas with which the agent is not familiar, enhances their professional status. In addition, telling a client that you are not familiar with their business shows a superior level of honesty and integrity.

Anne's situation is not unusual. The ethical problems here include her lack of general knowledge in commercial insurance and lack of specific knowledge of the survey industry. Additionally, she was being asked to write a "claims made" policy, with which she is not familiar. Instead of making a joke of not knowing what a theodolite is (a surveying tool that measures elevation and direction), she should have acknowledged her lack of depth in that industry and asked the prospect for help in defining terms and equipment usage. Yet, not wanting to appear foolish or inexperienced, her personal pride overcame her judgment. The result is a misrepresentation of her abilities to serve the consumer.

Her boss, Jim Carlson, is also involved in the situation by not taking the time to review the possible coverages needed for a survey firm, by not suggesting that Anne delay the meeting until more information could be gathered and by not suggesting that they both talk to an underwriter to glean as much information as possible about writing such a risk. In some states, Jim might be considered vicariously guilty of misrepresentation because he allowed Anne to continue on this account without adequate knowledge of the risk. Jim has little or no knowledge of the surveying industry. He doesn't direct Anne to the insurance underwriters who could tell her whether the companies the Carlson Agency represents have the desire or capability to quote on a surveying company. Although the underwriters could walk Anne through the initial underwriting and application process, three weeks is usually not enough time for most underwriters to carefully analyze and provide a quote on an unusual risk.

In this situation, Jim should have called RJ and Leon and suggested that the risk not be quoted through his office because the producers lack the industry knowledge, the time frame for such a complex quotation is too short and/or their insurers do not wish to write surveying businesses. (If it is true that the insurers cannot write the risk, caution should be used to assure RJ and Leon that their company is not being discriminated against because it's *their* company. The risk is simply one that does not fall within the "normal range" of expected losses written by the insurers represented by the Carlson Agency.)

Anne should have acknowledged her lack of expertise in the surveying industry when first approached by RJ. She might have suggested an initial meeting with Jim and another meeting with experts from the insurance company (underwriters, loss control specialists, account representatives) and Leon's risk manager and/or attorney to determine needed coverage. Without adequate knowledge, Anne will be unable to provide a comprehensive quotation for the new business and, if RJ or Leon tells other clients about her misrepresentation of her expertise, she may even lose some of the business she currently writes.

***** *Analysis*

Ethical Issue Number Five

This is a very difficult situation in which many agents find themselves at least once in their careers. How much information can they disclose to the client about what another agent is doing, the program he or she is offering and the possibility of a violation of the law?

As a licensed insurance agent, Andy must not give any impression of the character or moral integrity of a competitor. That is a violation of many state laws concerning defamation of an agent or company. This ethical issue is compounded by the knowledge that Charlie may be, even unintentionally, redlining, or discriminating against the Sanchezes by not offering them the POP program because their rental units are in a racially mixed area. (We will return to Charlie in a moment.) Yet, even at the higher LRP premium, the Sanchezes would be getting a better deal with Charlie's program. Unfortunately, there is no easy answer to this situation for Andy. He must weigh his personal values and integrity with the facts of the situation and determine how the law would view the entire transaction. He might consult either an underwriter for one of the companies he has worked with in the past or the insurance department in his state.

Charlie also has a problem. Is he discriminating against the Sanchezes? The simple answer is "yes." Assume that he is not selling the less expensive POP program only to middle-class neighborhoods; he occasionally offers a POP quote to landlords in lower-income neighborhoods. The fact that he can *choose* which program to sell to whom is the key in this issue. The decision as to which program to use is arbitrary and not based on actuarial data. In addition, there is the strong possibility that New World and/or Charlie discriminate by neighborhood, technically called redlining. Two individuals of the same class and risk status should not be charged different rates for the same coverage. This is not only a possible violation of state laws, but also of federal antidiscrimination laws. This is a line that clearly cannot be crossed.

Finally, New World may be asked by the insurance department to justify the rates and commissions charged. If there is no difference in underwriting criteria, costs or possibility of loss, the rates for the LRP program may be considered excessive, inadequate or unfairly discriminatory. New World Insurance, as well as the National Agency, could be subject to fines, cease and desist orders and/or certificate of authority and license suspension or revocation.

Analysis

Ethical Issue Number Six

As with many new agents, Susan's enthusiasm has caused some misjudgments in her sales approach and policy information. There are four possible ethical and legal violations within this short scenario.

1. Misrepresentation—The HO-3 policy does not include "all risk" coverage for property. It is more correctly called "open perils" coverage because the policy contains certain exclusions and limitations on coverage. Personal property is covered on a named perils basis; however, open perils coverage may be added by endorsement.

2. Rebating—Though not a direct violation of law in many states, the extension of credit can be perceived as an inducement to purchase by offering an interest-free loan Even if interest is charged, this still can be considered rebating in many jurisdictions.

   The housewarming gift may be the toughest problem in this case. Although the intent of the gift is a "housewarming" present, it is the *perception* of the reason for the gift that will determine whether it is considered rebating or an inducement to purchase insurance. Many believe that the timing of such a gift is the determining factor; however, this is not always so. Whether the gift is given before, immediately after or sometime in the future to assure that insurance coverage will be provided, some states will consider the gift to be rebating.

3. Commingling—Collected premiums and personal funds must be maintained in separate accounts. The depositing of a premium check (even if it is a deposit on premium) in a personal or general business account is an apparent legal violation.

4. Coercion—Susan agreed to help the Leats *only* if they agreed to let her write their auto coverage. They needed homeowners insurance so they agreed to let Susan write their auto insurance. In most cases, such action—forcing a client to agree to an agent's terms—is considered illegal and unethical.

Susan's supervisor should not curtail Susan's enthusiasm, but direct it with additional training and advice. Reminding her that commingling and rebating are violations of state law and that the contract does not provide all risk coverage for personal property will be an important lesson for Susan and one she will not forget. Susan should immediately correct the Leats' impression about their homeowners coverage.

Codes of Ethics

CODE of ETHICS *

Independent Insurance Agents of America

I believe in the insurance business and its future, and that the Independent Insurance Agent is the instrument through which insurance reaches its maximum benefit to society and attains its most effective distribution.

I will do my part to uphold and build the Independent Agency System which has developed insurance to its present fundamental place in the economic fabric of our nation. To my fellow members of the Independent Insurance Agents of America, I pledge myself always to support right principles and oppose bad practices in the business.

I believe that these three have their distinct rights in our business: first, the Public; second, the Insurance Companies; and third, the Independent Insurance Agents, and that the rights of the Public are paramount.

To the public

I regard the insurance business as an honorable occupation and believe that it affords me a distinct opportunity to serve society.

I will strive to render the full measure of service that would be expected from an Independent Insurance Agent.

I will analyze the insurance needs of my clients, and to the best of my ability, recommend the coverage to suit those needs.

I will endeavor to provide the public with a better understanding of insurance.

I will work with the national, state, and local authorities to heighten safety and reduce loss in my community.

I will take an active part in the recognized civic, charitable, and philanthropic movements which contribute to the public good of my community.

To the companies

I will respect the authority vested in me to act on their behalf.

I will use care in the selection of risks, and do my utmost to merit the confidence of my companies by providing them with the fullest creditable information for effective underwriting, nor will I withhold information that may be detrimental to my companies' sound risk taking.

I will expect my companies to give to me the same fair treatment that I give to them.

To fellow members

I pledge myself to maintain friendly relations with other agencies in my community. I will compete with them on an honorable and fair basis, make no false statements, nor any misrepresentation or omission of facts.

I will adhere to a strict observance of all insurance laws relative to the conduct of my business.

I will work with my fellow Independent Insurance Agents for the betterment of the insurance business.

Realizing that only by unselfish service can the insurance industry have the public confidence it merits, I will at all times seek to elevate the standards of my occupation by governing all my business and community relations in accordance with the provisions of this Code and by inspiring others to do likewise.

---

* Reproduced with permission from the Independent Insurance Agents of America.

American Institute for Chartered Property and Casualty Underwriters

*Code of Professional Ethics**

Canons and Rules

Canon 1
CPCUs Should Endeavor at All Times to Place the Public Interest Above Their Own.

Rules of Professional Conduct

R1.1 A CPCU has a duty to understand and abide by all *Rules* of conduct which are prescribed in the Code of Professional Ethics of the American Institute.

R1.2 A CPCU shall not advocate, sanction, participate in, cause to be accomplished, otherwise carry out through another, or condone any act which the CPCU is prohibited from performing by the *Rules* of this *Code*.

Canon 2
CPCUs Should Seek Continually to Maintain and Improve Their Professional Knowledge, Skills, and Competence.

Rules of Professional Conduct

R2.1 A CPCU shall keep informed on those technical matters that are essential to the maintenance of the CPCU's professional competence in insurance, risk management, or related fields.

Canon 3
CPCUs Should Obey All Laws and Regulations, and Should Avoid Any Conduct or Activity Which Would Cause Unjust Harm to Others.

Rules of Professional Conduct

R3.1 In the conduct of business or professional activities, a CPCU shall not engage in any act or omission of a dishonest, deceitful, or fraudulent nature.

R3.2 A CPCU shall not allow the pursuit of financial gain or other personal benefit to interfere with the exercise of sound professional judgment and skills.

R3.3 A CPCU will be subject to disciplinary action for the violation of any law or regulation, to the extent that such violation suggests the likelihood of professional misconduct in the future.

Canon 4
CPCUs Should Be Diligent in the Performance of Their Occupational Duties and Should Continually Strive to Improve the Functioning of the Insurance Mechanism.

Rules of Professional Conduct

R4.1 A CPCU shall competently and consistently discharge his or her occupational duties.

R4.2 A CPCU shall support efforts to effect such improvements in claims settlement, contract design, investment, marketing, pricing, reinsurance, safety engineering,

---

*Reprinted with permission from the American Institute for Chartered Property Casualty Underwriters

underwriting, and other insurance operations as will both inure to the benefit of the public and improve the overall efficiency with which the insurance mechanism functions.

Canon 5
CPCUs Should Assist in Maintaining and Raising Professional Standards in the Insurance Business.

Rules of Professional Conduct

R5.1 A CPCU shall support personnel policies and practices which will attract qualified individuals to the insurance business, provide them with ample and equal opportunities for advancement, and encourage them to aspire to the highest levels of professional competence and achievement.

R5.2 A CPCU shall encourage and assist qualified individuals who wish to pursue CPCU or other studies which will enhance their professional competence.

R5.3 A CPCU shall support the development, improvement, and enforcement of such laws, regulations, and codes as will foster competence and ethical conduct on the part of all insurance practitioners and inure to the benefit of the public.

R5.4 A CPCU shall not withhold information or assistance officially requested by appropriate regulatory authorities who are investigating or prosecuting any alleged violation of the laws or regulations governing the qualifications or conduct of insurance practitioners.

Canon 6
CPCUs Should Strive to Establish and Maintain Dignified and Honorable Relationships with Those Whom They Serve, with Fellow Insurance Practitioners, and with Members of Other Professions.

Rules of Professional Conduct

R6.1 A CPCU shall keep informed on the legal limitations imposed upon the scope of his or her professional activities.

R6.2 A CPCU shall not disclose to another persona any confidential information entrusted to, or obtained by, the CPCU in the course of the CPCU's business or professional activities, unless a disclosure of such information is required by law or is made to a person who necessarily must have the information in order to discharge legitimate occupational or professional duties.

R6.3 In rendering or proposing to render professional services for others, a CPCU shall not knowingly misrepresent or conceal any limitations on the CPCU's ability to provide the quantity or quality of professional services required by the circumstances.

Canon 7
CPCUs Should Assist in Improving the Public Understanding of Insurance and Risk Management.

Rules of Professional Conduct

R7.1 A CPCU shall support efforts to provide members of the public with objective information concerning their risk management and insurance needs, and the products, services, and techniques which are available to meet their needs.

R7.2 A CPCU shall not misrepresent the benefits, costs, or limitations of any risk management technique or any product or service of an insurer.

Canon 8
CPCUs Should Honor the Integrity and Respect the Limitations Placed upon the Use of the CPCU Designation.

Rules of Professional Conduct

R8.1 A CPCU shall use the CPCU designation and the CPCU key only in accordance with the relevant GUIDELINES promulgated by the American Institute.

R8.2 A CPCU shall not attribute to the mere possession of the designation depth or scope of knowledge, skills, and professional capabilities greater than those demonstrated by successful completion of the CPCU program.

R8.3 A CPCU shall not make unfair comparisons between a person who holds the CPCU designation and one who does not.

R8.4 A CPCU shall not write, speak, or act in such a way as to lead another reasonably to believe the CPCU is officially representing the American Institute, unless the CPCU has been duly authorized to do so by the American Institute.

Canon 9
CPCUs Should Assist in Maintaining the Integrity of the *Code of Professional Ethics*.

Rules of Professional Conduct

R9.1 A CPCU shall not initiate or support the CPCU candidacy of any individual known by the CPCU to engage in business practices which violate the ethical standards prescribed by this *Code*.

R9.2 A CPCU possessing unprivileged information concerning an alleged violation of this *Code* shall, upon request, reveal such information to the tribunal or other authority empowered by the American Institute to investigate or act upon the alleged violation.

R9.3 A CPCU shall report promptly to the American Institute any information concerning the use of the CPCU designation by an unauthorized person.